Book Pre-Launch Marketing

By Lawrence Harte
Drew Becker

LearnQIC Publishing
1105 Walnut Street, Suite 160-25
Cary, NC 27511 USA
Telephone: +1.919.301.0109
email: info@LearnQIC.com
web: www.LearnQIC.com

LearnQIC

LearnQIC

Copyright © 2019, 2020 By DiscoverNet Publishing
First Printing

Printed and Bound by Lightning Source, TN.

International Standard Book Number: 9781932813227

About the Authors

Lawrence Harte is a tech media expert, book and magazine publisher, and author of 118+ books as of 2020. He has sold 310,000+ books worldwide and has set up and tested 100+ ways to promote and sell books ranging from traditional book distribution to customized branded books. He has run specialty retail bookstores at 90+ trade shows and conferences worldwide. As a magazine publisher and conference organizer, he has promoted books to email and mailing lists. He has developed creative ways to earn revenue from books including selling reference resource links inside the books, creating company and event-branded versions, licensed eBook versions, and others.

Drew Becker is a multi-book author, book coach, branding, and book marketing expert. He is the founder and president of Realization Press, a book author consulting, publishing, media production, and marketing services company. Drew is the co-founder and runs the Carolina Book & Writer Conference (formerly the Triangle Book & Writer Conference). He speaks at many writing, publishing, and marketing events including Wake Tech Community College, The Holly Springs Writers Group, Enfield Book and Writers Exchange, Triangle Association of Freelancer Conference and more. Drew has authored several non-fiction books (many on book authoring and promotion) and is working on several fiction books.

Acknowledgements

Many smart people have helped us to create this book. Some of them gave substantial amounts of time to share their experience, answer many questions, and invite us into their businesses and shared their successful experiences.

Book coaches who shared their tips, content, and wisdom with us including Alice Osborn , Diana Needham with Needham Business Consulting, Omar McCallop with Galaxy Studios, Diana Henderson from Realization Press, and Joe Mehbratu with Mehbratu Coaching.

Special thanks to the podcast hosts and industry leaders who educated and inspired us. These include Joanna Penn with The Creative Penn, Dave Chesson from Kindlepreneur, Tim Grahl founder of Book Launch Podcast, and several others.

Thanks to authors who reviewed our cover design, contents, and gave us feedback guides, templates, tutorials, and other resources that are provided with this book. These include Buddy Howard, author of *The Husband Survival Guide*, Waceke Waamba, Kiesha Watkins, Divya Parekh, Dori Staehle, and others.

Table of Contents

Chapter 1

Book Pre-Launch Marketing

Book Pre-Launch Marketing is the promotion of a book that is to be published in the future. Book Pre-Launch promotion has some differences and challenges from and key advantages over marketing a book that has already been released.

Authors, marketers, publishers, and others involved in the book production, distribution and topic areas can do Book Pre-Launch Marketing. Understanding Book Pre-Launch Marketing options, their typical results, and how to do them can help you to promote and sell your book and earn additional money before publishing it.

Book Pre-Launch Marketing Benefits

Book authors can do Pre-Launch Marketing to earn from book pre-sales and additional funds, rapidly get publicity and credibility, and find and insert additional media into their books. During the Pre-Launch marketing process, authors can make new connections with experts and book buyers, get review feedback for book updating, and use lists and other media to achieve #1 best seller status on Amazon and with other retailers.

Pre-Sales Money

Authors and publishers can earn money from the pre-sales, book content and marketing sponsorships and earn money from the sale of related products and services.

Books can be sold on the author's website, through crowdfunding platforms, and through prep-orders on Amazon and other online retailers. Authors can sell sponsorships to companies to include product information in the book, include references in book promotion media posts, and give away books in return for getting book buyer contact information. Authors can earn money through the sale of related products and services that include affiliate referral commissions, promotion partner deals, and book branded logo merchandise.

Rapid Publicity & Credibility

By doing just a few Book Pre-Launch Marketing activities, authors can rapidly get their books and name to become quickly discoverable on search engines and other media channels. The listings in search results listings will start showing up with the searches for the book title. With continued Pre-Launch marketing activities, book search results will come up when people search for key book topic, keywords, phrases, questions, and other book related topics.

Additional Book Media

Authors can contact marketing communication people at companies to request photos and other media such as applications and case studies. Company marketing communication people are usually listed at the bottom of press releases along with their contact information. Call and ask them for photos and additional references such as white papers, tutorials, and case studies. You can describe and provide links to these references as part of your book marketing materials.

New Connections

Pre-Launch marketing activities help authors to make new contacts and relationships with media professionals, subject matter experts, and qualified book readers. After requesting photos and media for your book from company marketing people or their publicity agents, you can connect with them on LinkedIn and develop relationships. Ask them to refer you to subject matter experts in their company who can review what you include in your book to ensure it is technically correct. To get qualified candidate book readers to interview, join and participate with discussion groups, you can send direct requests to group members and/or post requests for book reviewers on book topic-related discussion groups. Posting book reviewer request messages will quickly provide several people for these communications.

Book Reviews and Feedback

Book Pre-Launch Marketing activities enable authors to get feedback on topics in and sections of the book. Provide short sections of the book to new connections and pre-sale book buyers. The book review process starts by sending short book review request messages to new author connections. Personalize the review request message with a key skill the person has that you find on their LinkedIn profile or through other online information. Send short sections of the book to reviewers, typically 10 to 20 pages. Offer to include their name in the acknowledgement section of the book in return for their help.

#1 Best Seller Status

Authors can usually achieve #1 best seller status in multiple places for specific book categories with a relatively small number of book sales. To get best seller book status, authors should develop a book pre-sale list and send a pre-sale email "book available now" message when the book is launched. The author or publisher selects at least one book category for online retailers such as Amazon that does not have much competition. The pre-sale email message can include a pre-purchase incentive such as an additional guide, templates, or other materials if the person orders the book when it is launched.

Rapid Book Publicity & Credibility

Doing some simple Book Pre-Launch Marketing activities can get future books quickly listed in search engines. Sometimes within hours!

Pre-Launch Surprise #1 – Rapid Publicity & Credibility

- Rapid Search Engine Listings
- Topic Expert Media
- Influencer Mentions

Book Pre-Launch Marketing   © Lawrence Harte, 2019-2020

Search Engine Listings

By setting up and publishing on multiple media channels such as Twitter, Blog, Pinterest, YouTube, and others, you will fill search results lists related to your book. This is because search engines show a mixture of website types such as videos, pictures, blogs, social profiles, and others.

Topic Expert Media

By publishing valuable and original topic information on multiple blogs, groups, podcasts, and other online places, more people will discover you. By having multiple media posts and links to helpful resources such as white papers, tutorials— that you got from your media contacts—you will become recognized as a topic expert.

Influencer Mentions

Authors can get social engagement (likes and comments) from topic experts simply by asking for help. When you request help from and acknowledge the expertise of someone, they are more willing to help you. When your new contacts share information related to your book, you reach bigger audiences and their expert status gives you and your book more credibility.

Book Pre-Launch Content Improvement

Book Pre-Launch Marketing media contribution request activities result in getting more content for your book which results in you making a better book.

Pre-Launch Surprise #2 – Better Book Content

- **Contributed Media**
- **Expert Interviews**
- **Book Development Reviews**

Book Pre-Launch Marketing   © Lawrence Harte, 2019-2020

Contributed Media

Authors can request photos, diagrams, information, case studies, and other media that can be included or referenced in your book. The process starts by contacting media communication or public relations people listed on the bottom of press releases. It is helpful to identify specific photos and content that you are looking for and explain how you want to use it.

Expert Interviews

Authors can talk to subject experts to identify key topics and interests your readers need. You can connect with experts through discussion groups, get introductions from the media people you requested photos from, or contact them directly via LinkedIn. These experts can explain and provide details on hard-to-understand topics in your book.

Book Development Reviews

Authors can request reviews from people who pre-purchase the book and from qualified readers. Getting multiple people to review sections of your book (10 to 20 pages) during development helps to ensure technical correctness and can improve content flow and readability. Some authors may want to arrange for beta readers who will either read and comment on certain sections or read through the entire manuscript. Those who do the full read are helpful in finding repetitive materials, unclear or misplaced information and other problems that can be corrected before release.

Book Pre-Sales and Other Money

Book authors, publishers, and distributors can earn book pre-sales, sponsorships, and other revenues before publishing the book. Some of these money-making options are not possible after the book is launched.

Pre-Launch Surprise #3 – Pre-Sales & Other Money

- Book Pre-Sales
- Sponsored Media
- Crowdfunding
- Related Products & Services

Book Pre-Launch Marketing   © Lawrence Harte, 2019-2020

Pre-Selling Book

Authors can list their future books for sale and offer immediate pre-sale incentives such as pre-release versions or additional media. Books can be given as rewards for crowdfunding campaigns. You can list books for pre-order on Amazon and with other online retailers.

Sponsored Media

Companies and people can pay to include photos and content in the book, to be listed with sponsor URLs in author media posts (link value) and pay for resource download pages (sales lead generation).

Crowdfunding

Authors can earn extra money by running a crowdfunding campaign that provides rewards such as books, book supplements, book logo merchandise, and other items.

Related Products & Services

Book Pre-Launch money can be earned by promoting related products on the book Pre-Launch website that earn affiliate commission through co-promotion partnerships and by selling book related logo merchandise.

Book Pre-Launch Marketing Processes

Book Pre-Launch Marketing processes are tasks, activities, and procedures that you or other people can do to promote your book before it is published.

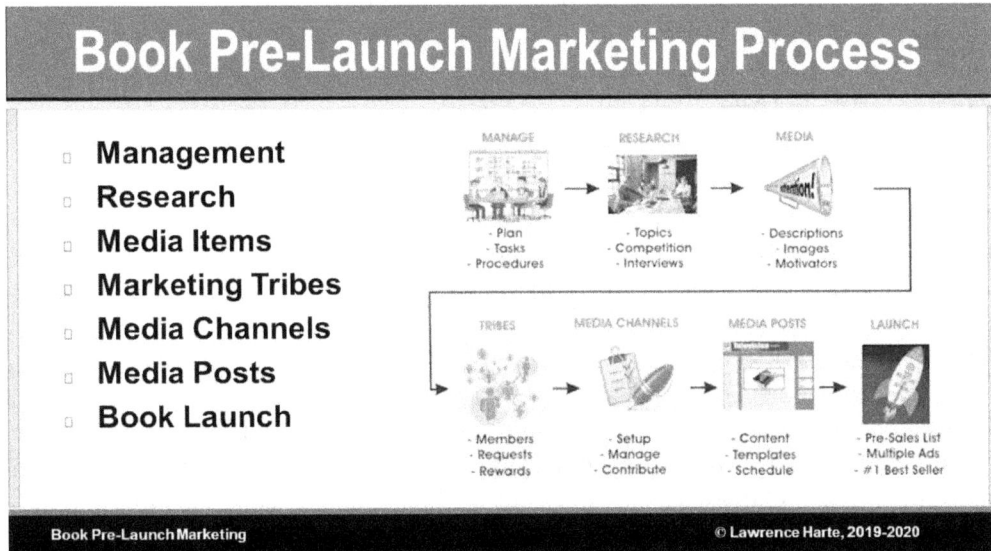

Marketing Management

Authors can simplify and organize Book Pre-Launch Marketing campaigns by creating a plan, task list, contact list, and other documents. Google Docs and Google Drive are simple and free tools to share book marketing documents and resources.

Research

Search, find, and review similar books, courses, and topic materials. Do buyer journey interviews with the top types of qualified book buyers and identify the key buying and reader motivators. While researching, continually add to lists of questions readers have, resources you can use and provide access to, and tips you discover that can help your readers.

Promotional Media

Create descriptions, images, and media items and profiles that can be discovered or shared with potential reviewers, contributors, and buyers. Create credibility by having promotional media (cover image, book business card) that you can send or share with people and can help motivate your new connections to help you.

Marketing Tribes

Invite some of your contacts to become members of book topic mastermind groups. These people can help you to promote your book by liking, commenting, and sharing media posts about your book. You can have multiple marketing tribe groups for different topics.

Media Channels

Register media channels that you own (your website and blog), setup media channels that you run (Facebook pages, your YouTube channel), or join media services where you can interact and contribute to discussion groups. It is important to setup and own multiple media channels in advance because it takes time for search engines to discover and add them to their search index files.

Media Posts

Convert your book content and research information into multiple, helpful media posts. Find sample successful media posts (search like your readers will search) related to your book topic (ones with many likes and comments) and use them to create media post templates. This will save you lots of time and increase the effectiveness of your posts.

Marketing Campaigns

Learn multiple ways (campaigns) that you can promote your book such as social media, discussion groups, email, and others. Download and use sample campaigns, templates, and procedures. Try several campaigns that match your skills, resources, and personality. Do these marketing activities for several weeks or months. It takes time to get discovered and to develop topic authority.

Book Pre-Launch Marketing Course

This Book Pre-Launch Marketing book has a companion course. It explains and shares successful Book Pre-Launch Marketing processes, management documents, competitive and book buyer research, key media channels and media post publishing, and 20+ effective Pre-Launch marketing campaign options.

Book Pre-Launch Marketing Process

The course covers key Book Pre-Launch Marketing processes that develop awareness, interest, and advice about selling books and related products and services.

Key Promotion Options

It explains over 20 ways authors, publishers, and marketers can do Book Pre-Launch Marketing. We recommend that you learn and try 10 to 15 of them and eventually focus on 3 to 5 which provide good results.

Media Channels

The course explains how to setup and use key media channels to attract and influence readers and book buyers. These range from book blogs and discussion groups to email marketing and advertising.

Media Posts

Learn key types of messages to create, how to craft them, and where and when to publish them. You will learn how to create and use media post templates to save lots of time and to make Book Pre-Launch Marketing more effective.

Marketing Activities

The activities section explains and provides instructions on campaigns to do marketing. Sample guides and media templates are included.

Book Pre-Launch Marketing Resources

The Book Pre-Launch Marketing course has companion guides, templates, procedures, lists of services, and other helpful Book Pre-Launch Marketing documents and media. These documents and media items are provided and continually updated by successful authors, publishers, and promoters.

To get access to the resource images and summary descriptions, go to LearnQIC.com/bookmarketingresources

To get access to fully-editable versions of these documents and media items along with sample text and additional instructions, register for the free Book Marketing for Authors course and go to the resources list. Go to: LearnQIC.com/BookMarketingforAuthors

Guides

Sample guides include instructions and procedures on how to do book marketing campaigns, projects, and tasks. Start with a sample procedure, adapt it for your own file naming system, storage locations, and tools and continually update your procedures as you discover better ways to do them.

Templates

Download templates, ready-to-edit media files, and layout guides that can help create promotional materials. Update the sample templates for your book, test them, and gradually update and replace your old templates with new, more effective ones.

Resources

Review and get additional resources such as lists of tools and services, sample plans, task lists, and other helpful media.

Success Examples

Book Pre-Launch Marketing resources include success stories, case studies, white papers, and other solution examples. Review examples that you want to try so you can determine which ones are likely to achieve your objectives (book fans, speaking invites, new projects, etc). Try multiple options that match your skills, personality, and resources.

Chapter 2

Book Marketing Management

Book Pre-Launch Marketing management is the coordination of process, media, and activities by authors, publishers, or marketing people to promote, engage, and pre-sell books. Book Pre-Launch Marketing starts by setting up planning and management documents, editing and prioritizing marketing tasks, and the creation of your pre-launch promotional materials.

Book Pre-Launch Management

- Marketing Plan
- Task List
- Contact List
- Procedures
- Files & Templates
- Reader Journey Interviews

MAKE IT HAPPEN!
WORK IT
PLAN IT
DREAM IT

Book Pre-Launch Marketing © Lawrence Harte, 2019-2020

Book Pre-Launch Marketing Documents

Important documents include a marketing plan (master reference), task list(s), contact list(s), procedures, and media items & templates.

Book Pre-Launch Marketing Plan

A Book Pre-Launch Marketing plan includes objectives, activities, and links to reference resources that are continually updated.

Book Pre-Launch Marketing Tasks

Book Pre-Launch Marketing management involves creating a list of activities, prioritizing them, and assigning responsibilities related to people including graphic artists, editors, and those in other roles. Start by creating a master task list with key marketing projects. Your master task list can include links to other task lists of activities for specific marketing project campaigns.

Book Pre-Launch Marketing Contacts

Setup a list of contacts for people involved in your marketing projects. This can be a spreadsheet that contain a list of staff, contractors, media agents, reveiwers, sample book recipients, and other people.

Book Pre-Launch Marketing Procedures

Create a procedures document that contains step by step instructions on how to do your marketing activities. These can include how to create and publish book blog posts and how to submit to discussion groups. Gradually create your procedures as you do them.

Book Pre-Launch Marketing Media Items & Templates

Create lists of your media items including photos, logos, sample images, media templates, and brochures. Include links in your lists to the media items. Setup your lists to allow you to have links to multiple formats such as low-resolution web and high-resolution graphics for print.

Book Pre-Launch Marketing Plan

Your Book Pre-Launch Marketing plan is your main marketing management document. It contains key objectives, audience personas, media descriptions, links to media resources (logos, images, videos), media channels, media post schedule, media agents, and other promotion activity plans. The Book Pre-Launch Marketing plan can be quickly prepared using a ready-to-edit sample Book Pre-Launch Marketing plan.

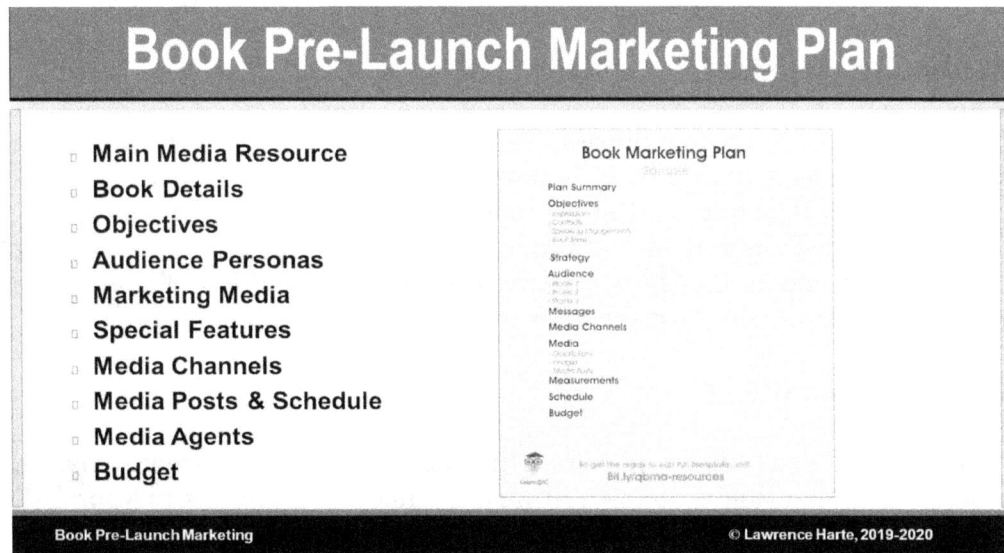

A Book Pre-Launch Marketing plan is more a worksheet because it is continually changing. It should be a single document that is used to coordinate your Book Pre-Launch Marketing activities and provide access to your latest and updated marketing information and media items.

Objectives

Book marketing plan objectives are the things that you want to achieve which you can control and eventually lead to book sales or other desired activities. Objective examples include speaking engagements, leads for consulting projects, and number of people added to lists. Objectives which are not directly controllable such as book sales can be divided into controllable objectives such as number of media posts, number of ad impressions, number of book reviews, and others that can be directly controlled.

Audience Personas

Audience personas are fictitious examples of people who want to read your book. Identify your top 3-5 audience types and their interests, pain points, and the media channels they use and trust. Do buyer journey interviews to identify audience priorities and dominant buying motivators (DBMs).

Media Descriptions

Media descriptions are summaries of your book that can be used with online retailers such as Amazon, book review sites such as Goodreads, book directories such as Bookbub, and other places that people may see your book. Create book descriptions in varying lengths from 25 to 500 words. Having ready-to-copy media descriptions can speed up the creation of marketing materials, submissions to directories, and creation of media posts.

Media Resources

Make lists of your media resources including book cover, logos, images, videos, and other media items and include links to the items in your list. Media items may have multiple sizes, formats, and resolutions so you can create columns in your list for multiple formats. For example – low-resolution (web) or high-resolution graphics (for print). When you have media items with different shapes or features such as square logo or horizontal logo, list them as separate items.

Media Channels

Media channels are any type of media presentation or distribution that allow for the exchange of media and information between the author or publisher, readers, influencers and other people. Media channels include websites, blog, email lists, and other services. Create a list of all the media channels that you will use to promote and share information related to your book. These may be channels that you own (website, blog, email list), some that you manage (Twitter, Pinterest, Youtube), and others that to which you contribute (discussion groups, etc.).

Media Posts & Schedule

Identify the types of media posts that you can create, where and how to process the content, and when and where to publish them. Setup media post templates to speed up your media post creation and publishing process. You can convert your book content and research information into hundreds of ready to publish media posts. Store these in a single file that is easy for you to access. As you publish the media posts, update the file and put a date and URL where the media post was published.

Media Agents

Create and invite lists of people who you use or can ask to publish information about your book or products. Set up rules for your media agents to follow such as ways to follow up with very positive comments and not respond to hateful or very negative messages.

Budget

The book marketing plan budget section identifies the estimated revenues, allowances, authorizations, and other expenses. Talk to other authors of books similar to yours to help estimate your sales.

Book Pre-Launch Marketing Task List

To manage many activities during book pre-launch, you must define, set up, prioritize, and assign tasks. A Book Pre-Launch Marketing task list can be accomplished with a single spreadsheet or an integrated project or activity management system such as Trello or Asana. It is important that all the people who are involved in your projects can easily access and use your project and task management systems. Using a Google spreadsheet to track book marketing tasks can be a simple way to organize, share, and track your project tasks.

Book Pre-Launch Task Lists

- Task Description
- Priority
- Due Date
- Responsibility
- Resource Link
- Task Notes

Book Pre-Launch Marketing   © Lawrence Harte, 2019-2020

You can (and should) continue to use your task list after you launch your book. Many of the pre-launch activities will be continued after your book is released.

Task Name and Description

For each key marketing activity, create a task name and short description that allows most people involved with your marketing tasks to understand what to do.

Task Priority

Create a priority for each task such as to be completed in a day (priority A), week (priority B), month (priority C), months (priority D), cancelled (priority X), or already completed (priority Z). You should regularly review, update, and sort your tasks.

Due Date

Create a date when the task should be completed.

Responsibility

Assign a person who is responsible for completing the tasks (initials). This may not be the person who actually performs the task. For example, creating a book cover image may be a design contest. The person responsible can set up the design contest on a site such as Freelancer.com, manage the communication with artists, and run polls to determine which cover is the best choice.

Task Resource Link

When possible, include a link to the task media item or project materials.

Task Notes

Include a column in your list that allows you to add additional information related to the completion of the task. This may be some key instructions, contact names, links to other resources, or other information that can help with the completion of the task.

Book Contact Lists

The development and promotion of books involves communicating with many types of contacts including editors, illustrators, reviewers, contributors, book buyers, and other types of people. Contact lists are one of the most important assets that an author or publisher can have for promoting, selling books, and engaging with fans.

Book Marketing Contact Lists

- Contact Lists
- Contact Types
- Access Permissions
- List Updating
- Communication History
- Email Service Provider

Book Pre-Launch Marketing   © Lawrence Harte, 2019-2020

Some contact lists require special sorting and management. You can have a mix of quick sortable contact lists (spreadsheets) and a master list of contacts (email service provider).

Contact Lists

Create an organized list where you and people you authorize can find name, email, phone, and other information related to people who are involved in your book production and promotion.

Types of Contacts

The types of contacts include book development team members, contractors, media agents, reviewers, sample book recipients, and others. You may use multiple lists (indexes of contacts) for different types of people such as reviewers, sample books, and marketing tribes.

List Access Permissions

Set up access permissions to your list or lists for people who need to find and communicate with your contacts. Permissions may be limited to specific contact lists such as web development contacts and access may be setup as view only lists or they may include editing privileges allowing them to update and add contacts.

List Management

Determine who has access to create, add to, and update the list. Plan to review, validate, and filter your lists.

Communication History

Set up your lists in a way that allows you and other people to find information related to a contact. This may be a sequence of communications such as requesting a photo for use in the book, requesting sponsorship, sending a section of the book for review and approval, or other communication activities. This can be as simple as putting it in the notes section of a contact or it can be a link in the contact list to a text file that includes multiple messages.

Email Service Provider (ESP)

Set up an email service (such as Mailchimp) that manages contacts, can send email messages to groups or types of people, and can track opens and engagements with email messages.

Book Pre-Launch Marketing Document Index

Book Pre-Launch Marketing can use hundreds of documents. To help find, sort, and share documents, simple indexes can be created.

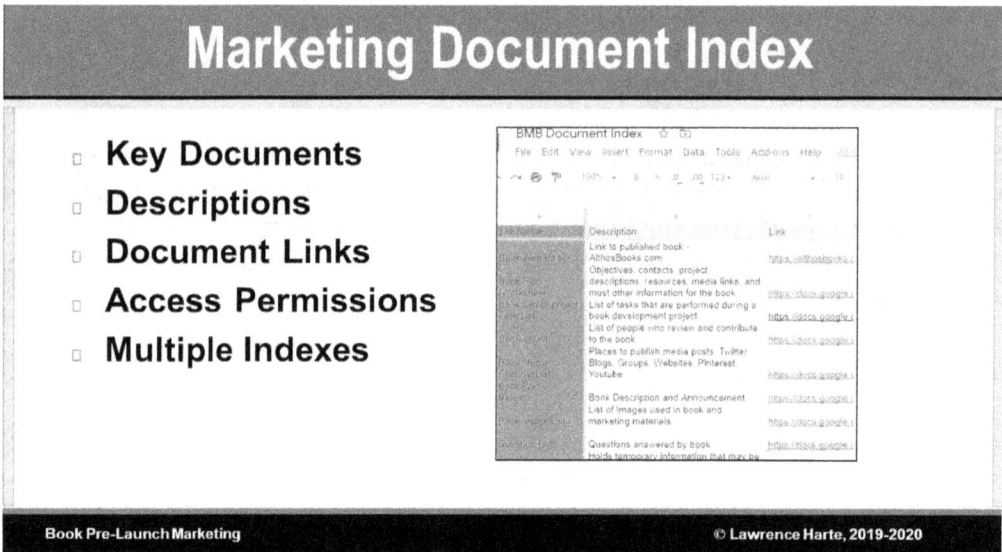

Marketing Document Index

- Key Documents
- Descriptions
- Document Links
- Access Permissions
- Multiple Indexes

Book Pre-Launch Marketing   © Lawrence Harte, 2019-2020

Key Documents List

A book can have a main document index (a spreadsheet) that identifies the book marketing plan, task list, media channel list, image list, and other key documents. It can also include links to other document indexes such as marketing, website, images, operations, and other document indexes.

Document Descriptions

Create short descriptions of the documents that define the topic and purpose of the document or media item.

Document Links

Include a link to the document, file, or media URL in the document index. This makes it easy to go to the media item after finding it in the index.

Link Access Permissions

Set up access permission to the document links in the index so only authorized people can view or edit the documents. For example, you may provide view access of the book press release to any contact but only provide editing access to editors and other developmental people.

Multiple Indexes

Create additional document indexes for other groups of documents such as marketing, business, operations, and media items. Your main index can also include links to the other indexes such as images, media content, and other documents. You can also create document indexes for specific people such as contractors, freelancers, and others.

Book Marketing Procedures

To complete Book Pre-Launch Marketing projects and tasks, many steps and processes need to be taken. Some of these processes are generic such as creating and editing images, and others are unique to the book author and the services that are used. To do marketing activities effectively, create and use marketing procedures.

Book Marketing Procedures

- **Marketing Procedures**
- **Gathering Sample Instructions**
- **Organizing Procedures**
- **Updating Procedures**
- **Sharing Marketing Procedures**

Marketing Procedures
Sample

Other Procedures

Book Directory Submission

Find and submit book information to book directory sites (BookBub, GoodReads, Radish, etc), book review blogs (category specific), and others)

Find a new Book Directory - use sample list or search to find

Add to Book Directly List
https://docs.google.com/spreadsheets/d/123ABC

Submit Book to Book Directory - use Email - *****@Submit@C.com

Upload Book Cover - image list
https://docs.google.com/spreadsheets/d/456DEF

Copy & Paste Book Descriptions
https://docs.google.com/spreadsheets/d/789GHI

Set Calendar Alert - 1-2 weeks to Review Directory

Copy Listing URL to Book Directory List
https://docs.google.com/spreadsheets/d/123ABC

© Lawrence Harte, 2019-2020

Book marketing procedures define file names, locations, and services that are used for projects. It is helpful to start by getting sample book marketing procedures that have already been set up and successfully used. They can be edited, updated, and expanded for your specific marketing activities.

Marketing procedures should be organized into sections that are easy to find and use. It is helpful to have the people who use procedures update them as necessary. Procedure document access may be restricted to specific people access for others may be provided on a view only basis.

Gathering Sample Instructions

You can acquire successful sample marketing procedures from other authors, join mastermind groups that share book marketing information and procedures, get samples from the web, or download samples from this book at LearnQIC.com/bookmarketingresources.

Organizing Procedures

It is helpful to create one main procedure document and include searchable headings for specific procedures such as blog posting and email campaigns. If the main procedures document gets too big (30+ pages), you can include links in the main procedures document to other procedure documents such as blog procedures or email procedures. You should be able to go to one place to find the procedure you are looking for.

Updating Procedures

Processes, files, and services change over time which require changes in procedures. It is helpful to have the people who use the procedures update them. After your procedures have been updated, get someone else to try and use the procedures without asking any questions. If they can't, the procedures need to be revised. Help any new persons to learn these changes and ask them to update the procedures when they are unclear. This do, document, and delegate process ensures that anyone with reasonable skill should be able to use your procedures.

Sharing Procedures

Set up access to your procedure document to allow your contractors, freelancers, and others to be able to find and use your procedures.

Media Files and Templates

Books and their promotional media files include many media files. It is helpful to create and use media file indexes and templates to save time and increase the effectiveness.

Media Files

Book marketing media files include photos, images, logos, press releases, a sales sheet, and others.

Media Formats

Each media item can have multiple media formats including resolutions, and digital file formats (jpg, png, tif, etc), as well as other variations.

Storing & Naming

Create and use a simple file naming structure that combines project codes and keywords that allow you to easily find and group documents.

Media Item Lists

Create media file lists (indexes) which include links to multiple versions of each format. Create a separate item for variations such as book logo portrait, square, horizontal, banner, and others. Include the media item name, short description, category (for quick sorting), media type (image, pdf file), and link to media items.

Media Templates

Create ready-to-edit media templates. An example is a photo file that includes the book logo and web address. This makes it easy and fast to create branded promotional media items.

Success To-Do List

Download Sample Documents

Download sample book marketing plan, task list, contact list, and other book marketing management documents. Update them by adding your book details including the book title, ISBN, descriptions, links to images, and other media.

Document Sharing

Upload your files to a shared drive (such as Google drive) and setup access sharing to allow your contractors and team members to have access to groups of documents.

You can get access to the resources described in this chapter by going to: LearnQIC.com/bookmarketingresources

Chapter 3

Book Pre-Launch Marketing Research

Book Pre-Launch Marketing research activities include reviewing competitive books, searching related book topic materials, and talking to potential readers. While doing your book marketing research, you can create several marketing resources including lists of questions and answers, reference resources (papers, guides, tools), and tips.

Book Marketing Research

- Competitive Analysis
- Book Reader Journey Interviews
- References
- Questions & Answers
- Tips & Suggestions

© Lawrence Harte, 2019-2020

Competitive Analysis

Competitive analysis involves finding and reviewing three to five books, courses, tutorials, and related media. Search like your readers to find similar books and resources.

Reader Interviews

Contact and interview 15 to 20 qualified readers to discover their key needs and interests, media channels they use and trust, and topic priorities.

References

While doing your research, make a list of resource items (papers, guides, tools, etc.) which you can use in your promotional media content and messages.

Questions & Answers

As you talk to experts and readers, ask them the types of questions they have or hear about your book topic. Create and continually update a list of questions that your readers search for and ask.

Tips and Suggestions

Create a list of tips and suggestions you and the people you talk to have for your readers. Become the hub for interesting, practical, and helpful information that develops value and emotions for your book topic.

Competitive Analysis

Book marketing competitive analysis involves finding, reviewing, and analyzing similar books and their promotional media. Identify key topics covered in multiple books that you should include, media channels that cover book topics, and key words and phrases to use in book and promotional materials.

Book Competitive Analysis

- Books
- Courses
- Tutorials
- Web Portals
- Media Channels
- Media Content

© Lawrence Harte, 2019-2020

Books

Find three to five books with popular rankings that directly compete with or are similar to your topic. Review their titles, descriptions, and special features such as additional reference materials. Look at their book reviews and determine which you would want for your book. It can be helpful to write sample reviews you want to get for your book and adapt your book content to earn those reviews.

Courses

Find three to five popular courses that have a high number of students and have the same or similar topic to your book. Review their titles, descriptions, course outline topics, comments, and reviews. Look for mentions of tools or resources that are included with the course. You may want to include links to those resources in your book and marketing materials or create similar types of resources.

Tutorials

Find several tutorials or slide presentations (such as on Slideshare) with similar topics to your book. Review their titles, popularity (number of views), descriptions, and slide titles. Make a list of keywords, phrases, and image concepts that may be good for your book.

Web Portals

Find and review websites or platforms that are related to your book topic. Focus on ones that have high web visitor traffic. You can use a web traffic ranking service such as Alexa to determine the site popularity ranking. Identify the common topics and resources that are on multiple web portals. These are likely to be topics that should be included in your book and promotional materials.

Media Channels

Media channels share information between authors and readers. These include magazines, blogs, discussion groups, and others. Find which media channels cover your book topics. Identify the key topics discussed and shared on these channels. Make a list of keywords and phrases used on these channels in your marketing plan.

Media Content

Media content conveys information and emotions. Search like your book buyers would search and look for media posts, ads, or other topics related to your book. Gather sample media posts to use as examples for your book. Analyze the media content to make your list of primary and secondary keywords, phrases, key icons, and other elements related to your book content. Start to create media post templates for your book.

Book Buyer Journey Interviews

Interviewing the types of people who are likely to buy your book (qualified readers) is a key way to determine your book buyers' interests, where they are likely to see your book, and to discover their key buying motivators. Talk to 5-15 people from your top three to five qualified audience categories.

Book Buyer Journey Interviews

- Reader Personas
- Topic Discovery
- Invite List
- Interview Questions
- Benefit List Review
- Interview Analysis

© Lawrence Harte, 2019-2020

Reader Personas

Create book reader persona classifications that help you to find, communicate, and motivate book buyers. Personas are more than market segments. They are a set of characteristics that include job roles, typical activities, and other psychographic and behavioral characteristics. Give them names and images to make them easy to remember.

Topic and Media Discovery

Buyer journey interviews help to learn key reader interests, challenges, and pain points or desires for your qualified audience. Discover what media channels your audience trusts and uses (web search, groups, etc.) to discover and learn topic related information.

Invite List

People whom you interview about your book can be a mix of some close friends you already know (first interviews), qualified connections (Linkedin), and new invites (post book interview invites on topic discussion groups). Look for new contacts in places that your qualified readers visit or hang out such as discussion groups, forums, and meetup groups. As you send invitatioin messages and setup meetings, make sample versions of your email messages that you can copy and edit. Put them in an author scratch file that you can easily find and use. Update your messages as you discover more effective ways to invite and motivate people to do interviews with you.

Interview Questions

Buyer journey interviews should start with basic questions to learn the background (qualifications) and interests of the person being interviewed. Ask open-ended questions and take notes on key words and phrases they use. After discovering their topic interests, biases, and desires, begin to ask questions about book topics and key features. Make notes of keywords, phrases, topic interests, and related information about your book topic.

Benefit List Review

After you have queried for their background information, topic interests and viewpoints, show them a list of your key book benefits. Ask them to prioritize how important they are: 1 - not very important, 10 - extremely important. Ask them to provide some key reasons why these benefits are important.

Interview Analysis

After you have interviewed 15-20 people from your three to five top reader categories, review and compare your interview notes. Review the book topic priorities ratings lists to determine the most important interests. The book topics that share the highest ratings from all of your audiences are your dominant buying motivators - DBMs. Create lists of the keywords and phrases your readers use and which media channels they trust and use.

References and Resources

References and resources are additional media that your readers can discover and use when searching for and reading your book. While doing your book research, create and continually add to a list (a spreadsheet) of useful and helpful resources you create (templates) and ones you find. These include lists of similar books, guides, white papers, tools, services, and other helpful media that can be included as links in promotional messages for your book.

Key Book Topics

Find helpful resources related to your book topic, create short descriptions, create categories that help you to organize related resources, and include links to the resources. You can organize resources by category and publish lists of resource types on your website, blog, and to groups or other places that attract potential book buyers.

Tools and Services Lists

Create lists of key tools, services, companies, and other items that can help your readers. List seekers are highly motivated to get information or stories related to their search. Create a master directory list you can use, find, and sort, to create lists.

Samples and Templates

Create or collect helpful documents and materials such as plans, stories, and other materials that can help the reader use or get a better experience from the book. Create media templates for readers to use to implement the book topic or so they can create media posts they can customize and share with their friends.

Examples and Benchmarks

Gather application examples, data, and stories related to your book topics and include credibility references for where they came from. Share examples, key benchmarks, or motivational stories on your media channels such as your website, blog, or social media channels. Include references to trustworthy sources when possible to add authority.

Topic Questions and Answers

Share book topic questions and answers in your book blog, discussion groups, and other media channels to attract and help your readers. Create these questions and answers while doing your book research and reader interviews and create and continually add to a list of questions your readers are searching for to use in your promotional media.

Question List

Gradually build a text file of questions and answers. Setup a companion spreadsheet that links to the text file headings that enables you to sort and track the use of questions.

Book Topic Questions & Answers

- Question List
- Searchable Questions
- Question Types
- Value Answers
- Helpful Resources
- Places to Publish

© Lawrence Harte, 2019-2020

Searchable Questions

Set up the question sentence format to match how your audience readers would search such as "Top Books <Topic>." Make multiple variations of your questions that include alternative keywords and phrases.

Question Types

Focus on creating the types of questions that your audiences ask or search for when looking to buy books like yours. Some questions have buying intent and others are just information requests. Buying types of questions may include How-To, The Same As list of solution options (list seekers are buyers), and implementation focused questions that are asked by people looking for solutions.

Value Answers

Provide some helpful information in the answer to the question. If possible, provide some hard-to-find value information such as benchmarks or typical results. Provide an example related to the question topic and, if possible, find a photo or image that relates to the question-answer benefit.

Helpful Resources

Include additional helpful references in the answers to questions. This may be a link to a resource such as a tutorial or story from another source. If you include a link to a resource that is not yours, you can contact the resource owner and let them know about your link. In addition to making new contact, the owner of the resource may be willing to promote some of your resources.

Places to Publish

Publish your book topic questions and answers on book blogs, discussion groups, YouTube, question forums, and other places. Asking for feedback and additional suggestions about questions is an easy way to get high social engagement value which can boost search ranking results.

Book Topic Tips and Suggestions

You can share book topic tips and motivational stories in your marketing materials, in conversations you have with readers, and in messages you share with your audience. While doing your research and having discussions with experts, ask for success tips and exciting stories. Create and continually add to a list of tips and suggestions you discover that your readers are likely to find helpful.

Book Topic Tips and Recommendations

- Tip Scratch File
- Tip Gathering
- Tip Sharing
- Tip Message Templates

© Lawrence Harte, 2019-2020

Tips Scratch File

Create a tips scratch word processor document (e.g. a Google Doc) that you can add tip concepts as you discover them. Create searchable headings for tip categories. Continually add and update your tips file. Review and update tips each time you use them.

Tips Gathering

You can discover tips by listening to topic information sources such as podcasts, tutorials, and other topic information sources. Talk with subject matter experts (SMEs) and ask them to share their success experiences with you. Become a tip hub. Ask for tips and offer to share tips. The more tips you share, the more you will get.

Tip Sharing

Determine a need before sharing book topic tips. Sharing unwanted or unrelated tips can be a quick way to demotivate people you are talking with. It is better to share tips one at a time when possible to ensure the maximum perceived value for each tip.

Tip Message Templates

Create ready to share tip messages that explain the tip, their benefits, and example if possible. Gradually update and improve your sample tip messages over time.

Book Research Success To-Do List

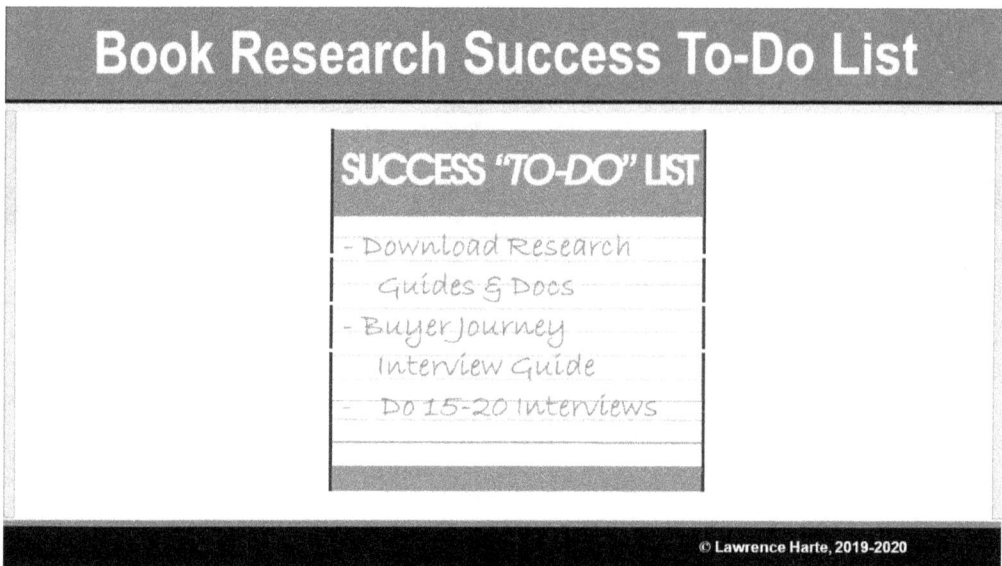

Download Research Guides and Docs

Download and update sample documents including competitive analysis, your buyer journey guide and sample messages.

Buyer Journey Interview Guide

Review the steps in buyer journey interviews and learn how to find, invite, and interview qualified reader candidates.

Book Buyer Interviews

Find, invite, and interview the key types of people who are interested in your book topic. Start with a few close friends to get familiar with your process, interview some qualified people you know, and then interview 5-15 new people you invite.

You can get access to the resources described in this chapter by going to: LearnQIC.com/bookmarketingresources

Chapter 4

Book Promotional Materials

Book promotional graphics and information are used to attract, motivate, and communicate with contributors, reviewers, and book buyers. It is extremely helpful to have some graphics and book descriptions before your book launch.

Book Promotional Media

- Descriptions
- Buying Motivators
- Cover & Logos
- Book Business Card
- Book Brochure
- Press Kit

© Lawrence Harte, 2019-2020

Descriptions

Create multiple length descriptions running from 25 words to 500+ words. Having these ready to use will dramatically speed up your marketing when you find places where you can list and describe your book.

Buying Motivators

Create a list of keywords, phrases, and needs that develop and trigger interest and desire for your book.

Cover

Develop a cover that gets attention when put next to several other covers and that develops topic interest and emotions.

Logos

Create small logo and banner graphic versions of your cover that you can use for media profiles and channels such as Facebook header, Twitter, Blog, and others.

Book Business Card

Create a book business card that you can give to people which includes motivational information and follow-up incentives.

Book Brochure

Create a single sheet that provides book details, motivational information, and ways to follow-up and get more information.

Press Kit

Setup an online press kit where media people can go to get images and information about your book. Make it easy for the press to find and publish your book information in their magazines, web portals, and other media channels.

Book Descriptions

Create book descriptions that match and motivate qualified readers to want to learn more about the benefits and value your book can offer them. Your description should share what your book can do for your readers and not be a summary version of your book.

Book Descriptions
- Problem Statement
- Shocking Factoid
- Pain Points
- Solution Promise
- Multiple Lenghts

© Lawrence Harte, 2019-2020

Problem Statement

Start your description with the main challenge (problem statement) or topic interest (key topic desire) that the desired audience has. Target audiences that can relate to the problem statement or story adventure will want to read more.

Shocking Factoid

Follow your initial statement with another, an unknown or surprising information value that helps to define or assist in solving their problem or provides an exciting plot promise. This develops reader interest and memorable emotional thought.

Pain Points

Provide 2-3 sentences that identify and amplify the unwanted difficulties or challenges the key problem or plot causes. This builds the reader's needs and emotional state.

Solution Promise

Finish the first paragraph with a sentence that explains how the content or solution will help or inspire the reader. Focus on the key benefit the reader will get from reading the book.

Multiple Lengths

Create descriptions of your book with multiple lengths; 25, 50, 100, 250, 500+ words. Start with the long format and continually reduce and rewrite. If your audience types are significantly different (such as technical and business or fantasy and scifi), you may want to create multiple descriptions for your book for those audiences.

Buying Motivators

Discover and describe the book buying motivator topics that have high value and emotional appeal to book buyers. Use these buying motivators in your discussions and book marketing materials.

Pain Points

Describe the bad things or uncomfortable feelings that happen if potential readers don't learn what is in your book. Help the reader remember or discover the challenges your book solves and the consequences if they don't learn or take action.

Book Buying Motivators

- Pain Points
- Keywords & Phrases
- Dominant Buying Motivators (DBMs)

© Lawrence Harte, 2019-2020

Keywords and Phrases

Discover and create lists of keywords, phrases, terms, and other text clips that trigger thoughts related to your book topic. These topic related words should prompt thoughts and emotions related to your book topic.

Dominant Buying Motivators (DBMs)

Discover and write the top three interests or needs that most of your qualified reader types want. These are your dominant buying motivators (DBMs.) Use your DBMs in the beginning sections of your marketing materials and early in conversations with potential book readers.

Book Cover

A good book cover gets a reader's attention, develops interest, and provides credibility that the book can help the reader with their challenges or interests.

Attention

Your book cover should stand out (pop) when placed next to 20 other books within a few seconds. Book cover attention typically comes from colors, shapes, and icons.

Interest

Design your cover to develop topic interest in less than 10 sections by including icons, images, and topic-provoking messages. Lay out your cover so the visual information sequence (eye flow) builds a value promise.

Conviction

Include images and information on why the book is likely to help the reader. This can be trusted icons, success examples, and book blurbs from respected people.

Desire

Use images and concepts in your cover that motivate immediate action. These images and messages should trigger desire for the information in your book.

Cover Creation

Book cover development options include using a graphics artist, cover templates, or running a cover design contest. Graphics artists can ready your book descriptions and ask questions about your subject topics to create multiple image concepts. You can use cover templates or stock photos that can be selected and modified for your book topic. Design contests allow thousands of artists to compete for winning a prize for the best cover design.

NOTE: One thing to keep in mind is that the front cover might display on a cell phone or smaller-screened device and appear the size of a matchbook or smaller. Too much information will not display well. Discuss this with your designer or consider this if you are doing the design.

Book Logo Images

Book logos are small images that represent the book cover and topic which are used for media channels, profiles, and promotional literature.

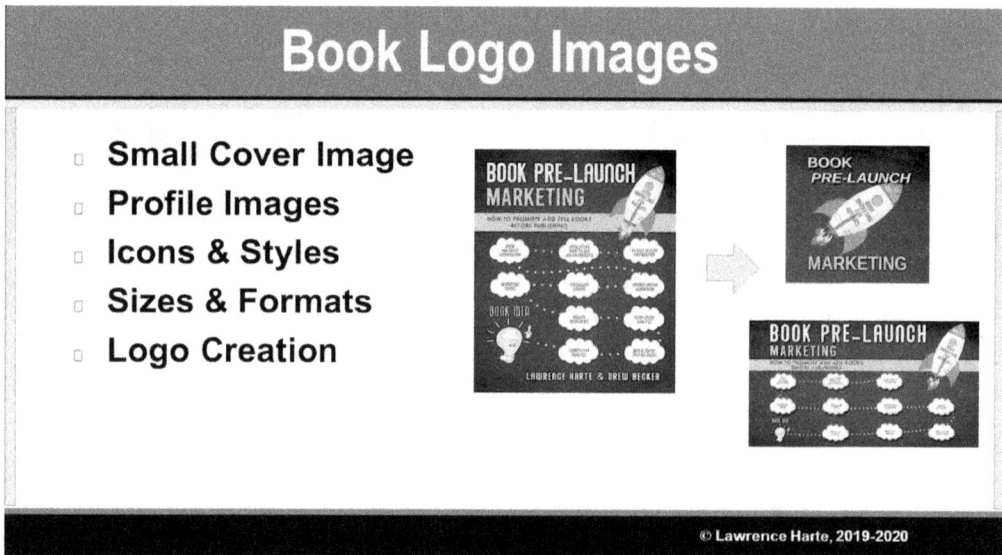

Book Logo Image

Create smaller graphic versions of your book cover in multiple formats. These graphics should look similar to your book cover and help the viewer to understand the main theme of your book.

Profile Images

Create images with specific sizes for social networks such as Facebook headers, Twitter, and others. Design some of them with large borders with the information centered because some profile images will be put inside circles. Use profile image names with fix sizes such as coverlogo400x400.jpg (400 by 400 pixels) or coverlogo250x100 (250 pixels wide by 100 pixels tall). Create some of the images with text that you can customize for media post images. This can be blog post topic or category image, podcast episode, or others.

Icons & Styles

Make your cover logo images recognizable as your book by including icons, colors, and styles that are used in your book.

Sizes & Formats

Create logos in multiple sizes and formats. Your logos should look good and be understandable when they are displayed in small sizes (thumbnails). Create a logos list that allows you to quickly find and get your logo images when you need them.

Logo Creation

You can create book logo graphics by copying and editing your book cover. Resize and remove some text and icons. You can have a contractor do this or run a design contest or freelancer project.

Book Press Release (Draft)

Book press releases share your book information with the media (magazines, shows, etc.), show up in book topic search results, and provide credibility for your book (it must be good if it has a press release).

Book Press Release (Draft)

- Press Release Types
- Discoverable Title
- Value Summary
- Buying Motivators
- Special Features

© Lawrence Harte, 2019-2020

A press release should be one of the first things you create when developing your book. Your press release describes the reason why your book will help readers. While your press release is likely to change during your book development, having a draft press release will allow you to share your book concept and get people to help you.

Press Release Types

Press releases can be created for media (to insert into newspapers, magazines and other media) or for consumers (for potential book buyers to discover which include influential buying messages). Media press releases include images and consumer press releases include links to book resources.

Press Release Topics

Press releases share news and new value topics. Your press release should describe the channels or interests your audience have and how your book provides benefits to your audience. While your book release may be your main press release, you can do other press releases for related book activities and new resources.

Press Release Content

Your book press release should include your book solution story (the news). This is comprised of an enticing title, a news value statement, and a book benefits summary description. Include special features, your contact information, and additional media (logo, book cover image, related photos).

Direct Press Release Distribution

You can publish your press release on your book website or web page and send it to newspapers, radio stations, TV stations, magazines, and journalists.

Press Newswires

Newswires publish and distribute press releases to journalists and news services. There are free newswires such as pr.com and paid newswires such as prnewswire.com and prweb.com. Publishing on an established and well used newswire (typically paid services) adds credibility and discoverability to your press release.

Book Web Page

A book should have its own website or a web page that the author or publisher directly controls. A book web page should provide book information, credibility evidence (reviews, testimonials), and motivational media that encourages visitors to submit their contact information (list building).

Web URL

Register a web address (URL) that includes the book title, book category, or other keywords if possible. You can point your web address (redirect it) to a website or blog that you create, to a Facebook page, or other web page that you can setup and manage. It is important that you own and can control your book web page without restrictions. If you share a social media page as your book product page and the social network (such as Facebook) decides to change the rules, you may lose your book product page. You may also want to insert affiliate links, sponsored media, ads, or directly sell your book which may not be allowed on social media pages.

Book Media

Include an image of your book cover, title, description, and key buying motivators in the main area of your book web page (above the fold). Your content should be enticing from a reader's perspective. What key solutions or exciting topics does it provide? The book details should be put lower on the page (like Amazon does) because they are usually needed after the reader had developed an interest in your book.

Sample Content

Include sample content such as table of contents (book topics), sample chapter or look inside, and/or other information that the person can view before buying your book. Include a special offer in your sample content that motivates your visitor to submit their contact information so you can follow up with them later with additional information and offers.

Contact Form

Provide a value offer that encourages a person to submit their contact information to your list. Include a simple contact submission form that only asks for a minimum amount of contact information: name and email.

Book Purchase Options

There are some easy options you can employ to offer your book(s) for sale and to accept payment on your book product page. These include inserting an Amazon product item to sell your book directly on Amazon. You can insert a Paypal order button and ship the book directly to the buyer. You can also install a shopping cart plugin to your website such as Woo Commerce.

Reviews & Testimonials

Inserting book blurbs, reviews, and comments can add influence and credibility that motivates buying. Include book blurbs and the names of the people who wrote them. Quote book reviews and their sources. If you set up comments and book rating reviews, you should be able to delete vulgar or inappropriate reviews.

Book Social Profile Pages

Creating multiple social profile accounts (pages) for your book on Facebook, Linkedin, Pinterest, and other social networks can be highly effective at reaching more people and getting listed multiple times in search results pages. You can setup several profile pages ranging from Twitter messaging to YouTube videos. You should at least own many social media channels with your name to prevent someone else from owning it and publishing things that are not good.

Social Profile Pages

- **Book Topic Discovery**
- **Profile Name Ownership**
- **On Platform Media**
- **Social Engagement Signals**

© Lawrence Harte, 2019-2020

Book Social Profile Pages

Setup 10+ book social profile pages (besides Facebook) to get multiple listings in search results for your book topic. As you add content to your social profile pages, your book will appear in search results more often as people search for related words and phrases.

Profile Name Ownership

Use your book title or keywords in your social profile name. It is important to register, own, and set up social profile pages even if you do not regularly (or ever) post to them. This will block other people from registering and potentially abusing them. Register them and set up your profile information even if you do not plan to post social content. Own your name!

On Platform Media

Adapt some of your book promotional media posts and publish them on your social profile pages. Social networks prefer their members to stay on their own platform. Convert and publish some of your media posts directly on social platforms (Facebook, Pinterest, etc.). Limit the number of off platform links you include in your social network media posts.

Social Engagement Signals

Set up a marketing tribe of qualified people to like, comment, and share your media posts on social networks. Search engines and platforms use social engagements to determine when and where to show search results and social posts. It is important to get qualified audiences to do social engagement with your media posts because they add more value.

Book Business Card

Create a book business card that identifies your key book buying motivators, has value triggering words, and includes a reference resource that motivates prospects to quickly take action. You can give your book business card to potential book buyers to help share your key book benefits while giving motivational follow-up options.

Book Pre-Launch Business Card

- 60 Second Book Introduction
- Key Reader Benefits
- Value Trigger Words
- Followup Motivators
- Multiple Versions

© Lawrence Harte, 2019-2020

60 Second Book Introduction

You can use your business card as a guide to interact with potential book readers. You can give them your card, share the three dominant buying motivators, and ask them if any of the topics (trigger keywords) on the back of the card interest them. You can share tips related to the topics they pick. You can then let them know about the resources on the card that you have made available.

Include the top three buying motivators that all your readers share as a common interest on the front of the card. Because these dominant buying motivators (DBMs) appeal to most of your audience, they are likely to develop interest for the right types of readers. This will allow you to start a discussion and begin a value relationship.

Value Trigger Words

Include 10-15 value trigger words on the back of the card that stimulate interest value for your readers. The goal is for your candidate reader to identify with two to three interests that trigger them to ask questions or take action. Have helpful responses and questions ready to for people who ask you about the trigger words.

Follow-up Motivators

Include an attraction resource title and link on the front and back of the card. Create and offer something that most of your audience would want to get such as a guide, template, sample story, or something enticing. Include a short link to the resource. A short link makes it easy for the person to type in the URL on mobile devices.

Book Brochure Sell Sheet

Create a one-page brochure sell sheet that helps distributors, retailers, and readers to discover, learn key values and details, and provide follow-up and contact information about your book.

Cover and Title

Include the cover to get attention and use a large title to help readers to identify the book and motivate reading for the right audience.

Motivators List

Include 3-6 book benefits readers will get from the book. This can include problems it solves or emotional experiences it provides. The goal is to develop benefit value and emotional interest.

Book Brochure (Sales Sheet)

- Title & Cover
- Motivators
- Summary
- Audience
- Outline
- Details
- Contact Info

© Lawrence Harte, 2019-2020

Book Summary

Create a one paragraph summary of the book that identifies the problem it solves or provides a story teaser along with motivational needs and interests and finishes with a reader benefit statement.

Key Audiences

List the top three to five types of audiences the book appeals to and what benefits they will get from reading the book.

Topic Outline

Include a list of sections or chapter titles. If they are long titles or topics, create short 1-3 word outline topics.

Book Details

Provide the identifying numbers (ISBNs), versions (print, eBook, audio book), size, formats, and other details for distribution, shipping, and ownership. Include retail prices for your book and its packages (print and eBook bundle).

Contact Info

Include a physical and online address contact information phone, email, and book URL information.

Book Press Kit

Set up an online book press kit which describes and provides links to documents (press releases) and media items (cover and photos) that can be used by the media in their publications.

Having an online press kit can help you to get more publicity for your book. Media professionals (such as magazine writers) have short deadlines and are constantly looking for information to publish. If your media press kit has descriptions, images, and reviews, it may be picked up (published) by magazines or other media publishers.

Book Press Kit

- **Press Releases**
- **Media Items and Descriptions**
- **Book Images**
- **Book Reviews**
- **Book URLs**

© Lawrence Harte, 2019-2020

Press Releases

List press releases about your book in text and pdf formats along with images. If you have published your press release on newswires, include the newswire links to your press releases

Book Descriptions & Author Bios

Provide multiple length versions of your book descriptions; 25, 50, 100, 250, and 500 words. Provide multiple lengths of author bios and author photos in different formats.

Book Images

Provide a list of book images and links to them in multiple formats. Include your book cover (front, back), some images that are used in the book, event photos, and other photos related to the book.

Book Blurbs and Reviews

Insert your book blurbs (recommendations) along with the names of the influencer. Include book reviews and their sources.

Book URLs

Include a list of the links where your book is available for purchase such as your own product page, Amazon, Barnes & Noble, and other online stores. Include links to book directories and key review sites.

Book Pre-Release Versions

Book pre-release versions of a book can be included as an immediate delivery incentive that motivates book pre-sales. This is typically a partial draft version that includes title, table of contents, and some chapter material. The pre-release version of your book can also include links to value items and special offers.

Book Pre-Release Versions

- Pre-Purchase Motivator
- Pre-Release Notice
- Table of Contents
- Book Brochure
- Sample Chapter(s)
- Special Offers

© Lawrence Harte, 2019-2020

Pre-Purchase Motivator

Create a partial version of your book and upload to online retail stores such as Amazon as an immediate item pre-purchasers incentive.

Pre-Release Notice

Include a big statement in the beginning of your pre-release book stating, "This is a Pre-Release (not final) Version of This Book." Include a statement that the content may change and there may be typos and other errors in this version. Include publisher contact information that helps a person to request the completed version if they received the pre-release version instead of the final version (it happens).

Table of Contents

Include a summary table of contents and a partial detailed version of your table of contents for the included chapters. This allows the reader to discover what they will receive in the future.

Sample Chapter(s)

Include sample chapters that contain valuable information. Include a partial chapter that ends in the middle of a key value topic (a cliffhanger).

Special Offers

Provide a value media item with an immediate download delivery offer. Use a link to a contact form to capture the name and email address of your reader that downloads the item. This allows you to build a qualified reader list which you can use to build a value relationship (offer other reference items) and to provide offers to other books or products.

Book Promotion Success To-Do List

Book Promo Media Success To-Do List

SUCCESS "TO-DO" LIST

- Book Descriptions
- Cover & Logo Designs
- Book Web Page
- Promo Media Items
- Pre-Release Version

© Lawrence Harte, 2019-2020

Book Descriptions

Create multiple length book descriptions.

Cover and Logo Image

Run a design contest to create attention getting influential book cover and logo images.

Website

Register a book web address URL and point it to a book web page or website that you control.

Promo Media

Produce book promotion media items including a draft press release, business card, and one-page brochure (sales sheet).

Pre-Release Version

Create a partial pre-release version of your book and include special offers and a contact request form.

Chapter 5

Book Marketing Media Channels

Book marketing media channels are any service or media platform that can share messages between book promoters and audiences. Media channels may be used to send (push) messages or they can be discoverable (pull). Authors and publishers can own or manage book marketing media channels that send or share information with readers.

Many book marketing media channels have a no-cost policy for publishing and distribution (such as Twitter messaging, blogs, discussion groups, image and video sharing). Some of the main benefits of publishing on media channels are discovery, influence, and better navigation to your book promotional media.

Book Pre-Launch Media Channels

- Purpose
- Types of Channels
- Media Channel Setup
- Media Channel Management

Messaging
Blog
Discussion
Image
Audio
Video

Setup & Manage 10+ Media Channels

© Lawrence Harte, 2019-2020

Media Channel Purpose

Each media channel should have objectives, scope, and communication strategy (frequency, post types). The focus of the media channel should match the types of people who use it, what content they expect, and how often they interact with it.

Media Channel Types

Media channels can be owned (completely controlled), managed (moderated), or contributed to (media sharing). The types include one-way (broadcast), unicast (direct), two-way (social), and response (submission and monitoring) channels.

Media Channel Setup

Search for and identify available media channels that have relevant category and keywords to start the setup of your media channels. Next, create the account, select the name and URL, setup and configure the media channel for publishing and distribution.

Media Channel Management

Media channel management involves selecting the media message topics, content sources, and how often you should publish to the media channel. There may be multiple people who can publish to the media channel (staff, contractors, etc.).

Media Channel Purpose

The purpose of media channels is to send or share messages to people or help them to discover your book, influence their mindset about your book or related product, and provide them a way to purchase your book or another follow-up activity.

Media Channel Objectives

Media channels are used to share messages with people at specific times to make them aware and influence their mindset about a product, service, or topic. The content (posts or media) published on media channels should be valuable to the audience, controllable by the sender, and measurable (sending and engagement results if possible). Key objectives can be the types, content value, and number of media posts that are published. You may be able to measure or estimate the number of people who can see the media (reach) and how often the media posts are seen by the audience (frequency).

Media Channel Audience

Media channels may be used for their existing audience persona types (such as TV show viewers) or recipients may be chosen (targeted) from a media channel based on characteristics (such as age, location, income, etc.).

Media Channel Reach

The number of people (audience size) that a media channel is exposed to is it's reach. Reach can be measured by the number of people who see your message (impressions). In general, you get more influence (engagements and ability to remember) when people see your message multiple times (greater impression frequency).

Media Channel Content

The content that is published on a media channel should contain topic related information (within the channel's scope). Media channel content may be sequenced to build awareness and change audience mindset. For example, announcing a book and then sending summaries of key sections in the order they appear in the book can build such a sequence.

Media Channel Frequency

Media channel frequency refers to the number of messages that are sent over time and how many times a recipient may see the same or a related ads. In general, it takes multiple impressions for people to become aware of your media post or ad, remember it, and take some action.

Book Media Channel Types

Media channels are communication paths between the channel owner or manager and others who can read, use, and/or respond to the communication. Media channels can be owned, managed, or shared by promoters. Media channels can be one-way (web pages) or two-way (discussion groups). You may own, manage, or contribute to media channels.

Book Media Channel Types

- **Media Channel**
  - Owned, Managed, Contributed
- **Media Formats**
  - Video, Image, Text
- **Communication**
  - Broadcast, Direct, Social
- **Response Channels**

© Lawrence Harte, 2019-2020

Owned Media Channels

You can setup and own multiple media channels which provide full control over the media publishing content and distribution times. Owned media channels include websites, blogs, email, and directly managed media services. When setting up media channels, it is typically a good practice to use the book title or topic in your media channel name.

Managed Media Channels

You can register and use media channels on other platforms such as Facebook, LinkedIn, Pinterest, YouTube, and many others. While you own the profile, the content you publish on these media channels must conform to platform content and use rules. It is a good idea to include your book title or topic in your media channel name and URL (as you do in owned media channels). Even if you don't plan to publish on some networks or platforms, it is advisable for you to register your name on multiple platforms to ensure you own your name.

Shared Media Channels

You can join and share book related media with groups such as Reddit, Quora, and Facebook Groups. When publishing and interacting on shared platforms, you must conform to platform rules, the media channel owner rules, and follow social rules from the media channel members. Book promotion on shared media platforms needs to be indirect. It is okay to share a book topic tip. Direct promotion (book offers and discounts) on shared platforms may get you banned from the group.

Broadcast Channels

You can send messages to groups of people (broadcast) to develop awareness. This can be an ad on a streaming radio channel or podcast, an email message broadcasted to book buyers (BookBub, etc), or any other media channel that can send messages to groups of people.

Broadcast advertising is called push (interruption) marketing because recipients are not expecting the messages. This means your ad needs to develop attention (stand out) and rapidly develop interest. Ads may be for branding (to develop awareness) or to motivate actions (product promotions).

Direct Marketing

You can send messages to specific people (direct marketing) based on their characteristics (profile targeting). Direct marketing allows for selecting message types or customizing your messages.

Social Media Channels

You can publish and respond to information on shared media channels such as social networks, groups, image boards, and others. Publishing on these channels must conform to the platform rules (no illegal items, hate messages) and social rules (unwritten guidelines setup by the members). Book marketing on social channels usually requires indirect promotion such as sample guides, reviewer requests, and other media that is helpful or is of interest to the members.

Response Channels

You can get or monitor communication from your audience on response channels. Response channels may be controlled (such as submission forms) or they can be passive (such as Google alerts).

Media Channel List

A media channel list (such as a spreadsheet) identifies, organizes, and provides guidance on which channels are available for your book promotion, what content is to be published, and how often it should be used.

Media Channel List

- Channel Name
- Channel URL
- Description
- Strategy
- Post Frequency

© Lawrence Harte, 2019-2020

Media Channel Name

Setup or join media channels that have names that relate to the book topic or title. The title should be short (1-5 words) and be easy to remember.

Channel URL

The channel web address URL should include title or topic keywords if possible. It can be helpful to include word separators such as hyphens or underscores. This can help people to quickly see the topic and it can help search engines to identify your topic focus.

Media Channel Description

Create a 1-5 sentence summary of the topics covered on the media channel and the range and depth of what will be shared on the channel. You may define the types of audiences that will benefit from the channel.

Media Channel Strategy

Define the strategy that you will use to start, grow, and maintain the flow of content on the media channel. This can include initial post topics and frequencies, member building campaigns, and volunteers for group management.

Media Post Frequency

Identify the types and number of messages you want to publish or make available on each media channel. For example, publishing 100+ blog posts over a one-year period that includes topic summaries, guides, lists of tools, and other topics. This means you should publish two to three blog posts per week.

Media Channel Management

Each media channel needs to be managed for content creation, publishing timing coordination, and use of media agents.

Media Channel Management

- Media Post Content
- Publishing Rules
- Post Scheduling
- Monitoring
- Media Agents

© Lawrence Harte, 2019-2020

Media Post Content

Make a list of key media post topics, content sources, and the formats (short, long, images, etc.) that will be published on the channel.

Publishing Rules

Setup media channel publishing rules and guidelines, media post creation and approval steps, and how to respond when the rules or messages require special handling such as highly negative feedback or hate messages.

Media Post Scheduling

Define the desired time periods between publishing on the channel (message frequency). You may start with a short time period between posts during media channel launch (such as every 1-3 days) and slow the publishing as the channel becomes established. Setup and use media publishing scheduling tools such as Hootsuite.

Channel Monitoring

Setup channel monitoring (such as Google Analytics) and a reporting review process that allows you to determine which channels are working and how to improve them. Monitoring processes can be manual (such as viewing the number of book reviews) or they can be automatically monitored using services such as Google Alerts. Setup time periods for review and setup a chart for achievements and results (such as the number of book reviews).

Media Agents

Setup services or media agents who can create and publish media posts. Identify which media channels they will use and setup channel access to allow them to publish on those channels. Create assignments and measurable goals for your media agents such as the number of media posts published each month. Create guidelines and rules that your media agents can use.

Media Channel Success To-Do List

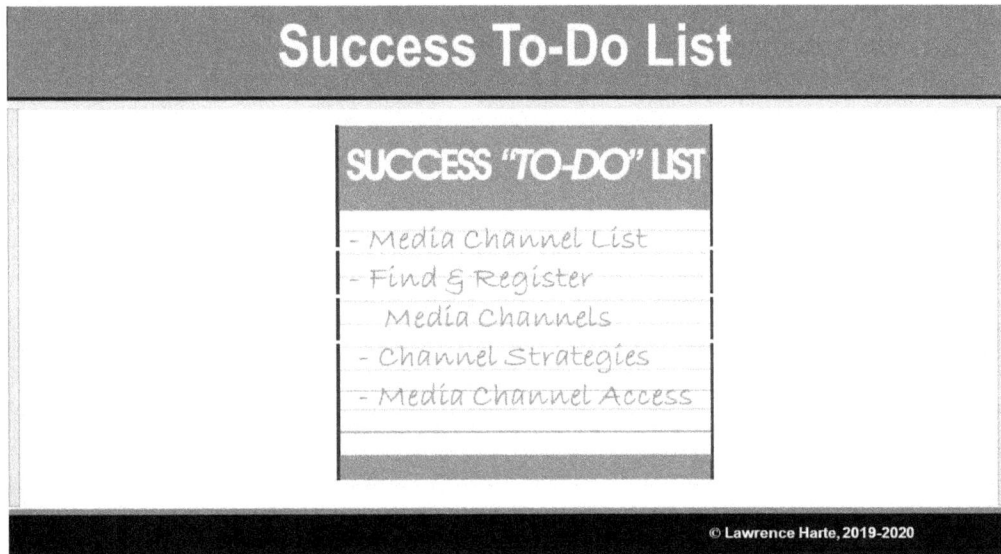

Success To-Do List

SUCCESS "TO-DO" LIST
- Media Channel List
- Find & Register
  Media Channels
- Channel Strategies
- Media Channel Access

© Lawrence Harte, 2019-2020

Media Channel List

Make a list (spreadsheet) of media channels that describes and provides links to media channels used for publishing book media and information. Include name, description, URL, strategy, frequency, and other useful categories.

Find & Register Media Channels

Search for available channels that match your book topic name or keywords. Register available channels and add them to your media channel list.

Channel Strategies

Define the purpose, content types, and frequency of each of your media channels.

Media Channel Access

Identify people who you allow to publish on your media channels (media agents) and setup access for them.

Chapter 6

Book Marketing Media Posts

Book marketing media posts are the communication messages (text, images, and/or videos) that are published on media channels (such as Twitter, Blogs, Streaming Media, etc.). Effective media posts can be created quickly using templates. You can use simple processes to create media posts from book content and convert messages into multiple media post formats (repackaging) allowing you to reach more people (bigger reach) through multiple media channels.

Book Marketing Media Posts

- Media Post Types
- Content Sources
- Post Templates
- Post Publishing

Publish 3-5 Media Posts each Day

© Lawrence Harte, 2019-2020

Media Post Types

Media posts types include announcements, guides, resources, lists, or other messaging information. The type of media post can determine the amount of buying or action intent a reader has.

Media Post Content Sources

Media post content can come from sharing expertise or experiences (original), summaries or insights into other content (curated), from repackaging book content (rewriting), links to other existing sources, or content contributions from other people.

Media Post Templates

Media post templates are guides that convert content into messages with defined formats. Media post templates can be created by converting original media posts into generic template versions.

Media Post Publishing

Media post publishing can be scheduled, tracked, and analyzed. Media posts may be published by media agents who have authorized access to publish on your media channels. It is helpful to have publishing goals and content guidelines for each media channel and for the media agents that you use.

Media Post Types

Media post types can be categorized by their purpose, message category, and buying intent. Key book marketing media post types include guides, resources, tips, and lists.

Media Post Types

- Message Purpose
- Content Types
- Buying Intent Value
- Media Format

© Lawrence Harte, 2019-2020

Message Purpose

The purpose of the messages which are published on media channels should match the audience interests and the scope of the media channel. Message purposes include announcements or news, navigation links, and information and media. It is advisable to create multiple media channels with different purposes. For example, you might have a book blog for topic related information such as guides and resources and a separate book blog for event information such as book signings, speaking appearances, and other event activities.

Key Book Media Post Types

Key types of book promotional media include topic summaries and guides, resources, tips, lists, and other categories of content. Topic summaries and guides provide topic explanations and implementation instructions. Resource media posts can identify, categorize, and provide navigation links to resources such as research, case studies, and other valuable information. Media posts may contain tips or lists such as a list of tools or services or a list of books similar to another book.

Buying Intent Value

The types of media posts strongly relate to the levels of buying intent of the people they attract. Media posts such as topic definitions and opinions tend to attract people who are in the discovery and learning phase with low buying intent. Media that includes research and application examples (case studies) can attract people looking to justify or verify their decisions. Guides, lists, tutorials tend to attract people who are implementing.

A good example of how content type influences buying intent is the differences in ad click rates for media types. DiscoverNet publishes multiple types of media; dictionaries, magazines, and directories. The ad click rate for dictionaries tends to be 0.5% or lower. Visitors just want to know what a term means, they don't usually want to buy it. Ad click rates in articles and tutorials tend to be 1% to 2%. Ad click rates in directories tends to be 3%-5%. In general, list seekers are buyers.

> **Ad Click Rates by Category (Buying Value):**
> Definitions - 0.5% - Low Buying Intent
> Articles & Tutorials - 1%-2% - Moderate Buying Intent
> Directories (Lists) - 3%-5% - High Buying Invent

Source: DiscoverNet Publishing)

Media Post Format

Media posts can have multiple text, images, videos, and other formats. It is usually possible to convert a single message into multiple message formats. Longer format content can be converted into many media posts. For example, a one-page article or section of a book may be converted to three blog posts. Each blog post may be converted into three discussion topics. Each discussion topic may be converted into three Tweets. If you use media post templates for the conversion, you can rapidly create 10x the number of reformatted posts in the time it takes to create one original media post.

Media Post Content

Media post content sources include:

- original experiences and skill sharing,
- conversions of book content,
- descriptive or explanatory related materials (curation),
- research materials (references) or
- contributed materials.

Media Post Content

- Original Content
- Book Content Conversion
- Curated Content
- Research Materials
- Contributed Content

© Lawrence Harte, 2019-2020

Original Content

Original content can be created from expert knowledge, application experiences, and from sharing hard-to-find information or benchmarks.

Book Content Conversion

A great way to generate many original content media posts is to convert segments of your book into media posts. Scan through your book, identify knowledge or story elements, and add them to your media post topic list (editorial calendar).

CAUTION!!! *Do not publish clips of your book content directly on the web. In addition to duplicate content search engine penalties or devaluation, publishing your content on the web may be discovered by online retailers such as Amazon who may delist your book. They don't want to sell what is available for free on the web.*

Curated Content

You can create somewhat new content by gathering, describing and sharing other related materials. The value in this curated content is the repackaging into a format that helps the reader to better understand or apply the curated content. Because the essence of curated content is already available, it tends to have lower reader and search engine value.

Research Materials

The reference materials (guides, tutorials, papers, etc.) that you discover during your book research can be mentioned and linked to in your book marketing media posts. You can let the owner of the resource know that you have referenced them and provide them with a link that shows your reference with a link to their material. You can also send them a connection request on LinkedIn or another social network to begin a helpful and co-promotion relationship.

Contributed Content

Another way to get high value content for your media posts is to request content from influencers and companies. Let them know you want to send or share their information with your readers—free publicity! You can ask them to provide a guest post for your book blog.

Media Post Templates

Media post templates are generic versions of message types that can be customized by changing tags and image elements.

Media Template Types

Create templates for different message types and formats including announcements, guides, lists, and other forms. Create template versions for different formats such as Tweets, Blog Posts, Pinterest, and others. Group these templates by categories in a templates file to help you find them when needed.

Template Format

Set up template formats so they are easy to find, copy, and edit. This can include text files that contain messages with ready to edit generic tags. It can also include image and media files in multiple sizes, resolutions, and digital media formats.

Sample Media Posts

Find and review sample media posts for books similar to yours. Search like your book buyers and audiences would search for your book topic. Use the successful (popular) media posts you discover as a guide to create your media posts.

Template Creation

To make media post templates, create original media posts, test them, and make generic versions of them. Generic versions replace words and phrases with replaceable tags. Replaceable tags can be descriptive words surrounded with brackets.

Updating Templates

Continually create and try new variations of media post templates. As you discover new effective media post types, add and use the newer versions. Keep the old versions as examples and as a backup in case the new versions become ineffective.

Media Post Publishing

Media posts can be created and scheduled for 6-12+ months in advance. This can keep your messages and topics fresh in the search engine indexes.

Media Post Publishing

- Schedule
- Channels
- Tracking
- Media Agents
- Publishing Tools

© Lawrence Harte, 2019-2020

Media Post Schedule

Create a media post topic list and organize it into a sequence (topic editorial calendar). Determine how many messages you can create (topics and media post variations) and which channels they will be published on. The number of messages published on each channel over time is the publishing frequency (posts per month, week, or day).

Media Channels

Identify the topics that will be sent on each media channel. The topic and scope should match the audience. Avoid publishing the exact same media post on multiple media channels such as on your book blog and as a guest post on a promotion partners blog. Duplicate content publishing can result in poor search results. Rewrite or refocus your media post variations so they provide some new original content value.

Media Post Tracking

Set up a spreadsheet or a service that allows you to track your media posts, requests to publish them, date they are published, and the URL to the media post. Starting with a simple spreadsheet will allow you to add categories which allow you to sort and see media post progress on channels and through people you ask to publish them.

Media Agents

You can authorize other people (media agents) to publish media posts for you. Set up a service such as Hootsuite that allows you to provide and remove media channel publishing access without having to share login information for each of your media channels with your media agents. The people who you authorize to publish on media channels should have online profiles (Linkedin, etc) that match your media channel topics.

Post Publishing Tools

You may want to use media publishing tools as the number of media posts and media channels become too large to manually control. Use scheduling tools such as Hootsuite or a WordPress blog scheduling plugin to ensure you have a steady stream of new media posts for search engines and people to discover.

Media Posts Success To-Do List

Sample Media Posts

Gather and review sample media posts on your book topic. Search like your readers, find successful examples (likes, share, positive sentiment).

Media Post Templates

Convert your successful media posts into generic versions that can be modified for other media post content.

Editorial Calendar

Create a list of key book topics, organize them into a sequence, and setup a calendar or use a publishing tool like Hootsuite to schedule your media post publishing.

Chapter 7

Book Pre-Launch Marketing Campaigns

Book Pre-Launch Marketing activities are groups of tasks (campaigns) and processes that are setup to manage the distribution of promotional messages and interact with desired audiences. This section covers 20+ Book Pre-Launch Marketing campaigns, their processes, and helpful tools. You should learn or understand most book marketing options, try 10-20 of them that are a good match for your skills, resources, and interest, and then focus on 3-5 that work well for you.

Book Marketing Campaigns

- **Campaign Type**
- **Marketing Procedures**
- **Campaign Management**
- **Sample Plans & Templates**
- **Marketing Tools & Services**

PRE-SALES   EMAIL   CROWDFUNDING   ADVERTISING

GROUPS   BOOK BLOG   REVIEWER COPIES

PROFILE PAGES   SPONSORS

© Lawrence Harte, 2019-2020

Promotion Campaign List

Start by reviewing and making a list of Book Pre-Launch Marketing types (campaigns) that have worked for similar types of authors and book promoters. Review this marketing list to determine which types of marketing fit your skills, resources, and personality.

Marketing Procedures

Create simple step by step instructions on how to do marketing activities. Write the steps you do for marketing in a procedures file or in a word processor file. Create your procedures as they relate to your files (tag which ones), tools (software), and services that you use.

Campaign Management

Create sample lists of activities (task list) and resources for each of your marketing project types (campaign types). Define how you assign, monitor, and update campaign tasks.

Media Samples and Templates

Create sample messages, telephone call scripts, media post templates, ready to edit images and videos, and other helpful resources.

Marketing Tools and Services

Setup and learn how to use key types of book marketing tools and services and lists.

Book List Marketing

Book list marketing is the gathering of contacts, developing profiles and relationships, and sharing information, requests, and offers to the people in your list(s).

Book List Management

- List Building
- Contact Profiles
- Messaging Campaigns
- List Bartering

© Lawrence Harte, 2019-2020

List Building

Book marketing list building involves attracting, motivating, and capturing contact information. You can attract and motivate people to share their contact information by providing a contact submission incentive. This might be offering sample books, companion content, contests, and any other incentive that attracts and motivates qualified readers to submit to join your contact list.

List Management

Setup an email list management service such as Mailchimp that allows you to store, organize, and send messages to a list of contacts. Email management services help you to create email messages and target specific people in your lists. This will allow you to select, customize, and track messages you send to your contacts.

Contact Profiles

The initial contact information you ask for should be limited to only their name and email. Asking for any other additional information such as company, phone number, or other information dramatically reduces the percentage of people who submit their contact data. You can do contact profile data building (get additional info) by providing additional value items (guides, stories, etc.) and asking contact requestors for additional profile details when they download them. Following up and providing value using multiple emails over time will build relationship trust and value. This increases the willingness of your contacts to share additional profile details with you.

Messaging Campaigns

Periodically send email messages (email campaigns) to your audience that provide value and occasionally provide offers. Value email messages include book topic related tips, guides, links to resources or references, topic related stories, and other information that is helpful or interesting. Offer messages may be a new book, a related product offer, or something that you want your audience to do. A good rule of thumb for email campaigns is to send value, value, value, and then offer messages. For fiction books these additional items might include character sketches, related materials such as recipes, pictures of characters, or family and relational trees.

When you send email campaign broadcasts, the email subject line should motivate qualified recipients to open the email and the email message should provide value related to the subject line (the solution promise).

List Bartering

You can rapidly multiply the number of people in your email contact list by 4x-10x by partnering with people and companies that have lists with the same types of audiences. This can be authors of similar books or companies that provide services to your reader types. The barter agreement operates when each list owner sends a message to their list. This allows you to review and approve the message you send to your audience. You should not sell or provide lists of contacts to your partner as it may violate SPAM regulations. Even if you did provide the list, it may not be good for the person or company that uses it. The sender's email address is very important. Email messages sent from an unknown sender tend to go to spam filter folders. The message you send to your partner list may be a book offer message or a high value resource such as a guide or free ebook. Sending a value offer message instead of a book offer message will likely have a much higher response rate and allow you to build your contact list. If you get new contacts, you can send them offer messages at a later time after you build a trust and value relationship.

Book Contributors

Getting people and companies to contribute information, photos, and other media for a book in development is a great way to improve book content, make new influencer connections, and to develop awareness and credibility.

Media Requests

To get photos or other content from companies for your book, you can send media requests to contacts on the bottom of company press releases. The media contacts on press releases are paid to get publicity for their company so they want to help you. As you contact and exchange messages with the media contacts, create sample media request and response email messages to save your time. It is usually helpful to request permission to use a specific photo or something else they recommend. Continually update your sample media request messages as you learn what you ask for and how you ask for it.

Subject Expert Requests

Getting subject experts and influencers to contribute to and review sections of your book will improve your book content. Contributors can generate great book promotion value as they are likely to give good book reviews and share information about your book to their followers. To get subject experts to talk with, start by identifying the types of experts you want to help you. Create a list of desired job titles, company types, etc. Search for these keywords on LinkedIn or on search engines. You can contact them directly, by using LinkedIn connection requests, sending messages through discussion groups, or through referral requests such as the media contacts you made when requesting photos or other media for your book. You can also post requests for expert help on topic-related discussion groups. When posting on discussion groups, describe the topic expertise help you are looking for, and offer to give a copy of your book in return for their help.

Connection Requests

Adding topic related connections to your LinkedIn or other profiles is a great way to develop authority and credibility. Shortly after getting a response to media and subject expert review requests, send a LinkedIn or other network connection request.

Use Permissions

To use contributed media in your book, it is important to get permission to use it. The process starts by defining the media you want to use and how you plan to use it. This can include using contributed media in your book and in promotional media content about your book. Ask for and get written permission. This can be as simple as getting a confirmation email from an authorized person (a company marketing employee) or through a use permission agreement.

Book Reviews

Book contributors are very likely to post positive book reviews, if you request that they post a review. Start by including the contributors name in the acknowledgement section of your book. Send a copy of the book with a "Thank you for Helping Me" inscription and signature. Put a sticky note on the acknowledgement page with an arrow that points to their name. Follow up 2-4 weeks after sending a sample book and ask the person to post a book review on Amazon and other places. Include a link to the book product page and either a sample review (if you know them well) or some suggested keywords to include in the book review.

Book Marketing Tribes

You can setup groups of people who are willing to answer questions, write book reviews, and publish media posts about your book. You can have multiple tribes (also called street teams) with different types of people. Make a list and track your marketing tribe members, what types of content they are willing to share, and provide them with simple quick requests, sample content, and URLs where you want them to post.

Book Marketing Tribes

- **Tribe Member Types**
  - Friends, Associates, Influencers
- **Member Requests – up to 3X**
- **Member Rewards**
- **Member Tracking**

Request, Give Sample Post, Ask Up to 3X

© Lawrence Harte, 2019-2020

Tribe Member Types

Marketing tribe members can be friends, associates, and influencers. You can start by inviting friends for your tribes who will be very flexible. While your friends may not have profiles that match your book topic, communicating with them will allow you to figure out the types of things you want your tribe to do, how to ask them, and ways to track your success. After you have gotten the basics of managing your marketing tribe activities, you can start to ask some of your qualified contacts to join your marketing tribe. These may be people you are connected with but don't know well yet. After you learn the kind of things your marketing tribe members want you to do for them, you can start to invite new influential people to join your tribe. At this stage, you should have a well-tested marketing invite message sample, value offer messages - what you are willing to do, and the types of requests you want your tribe to do - like, share, comment, etc.

Tribe Building

You should setup a list and build (add) qualified people to your marketing tribe. Identify key key member qualifications such as job role, experience, and other criteria. You may want to have a multiple tribes with members that have different profiles and skills such as sales, business, or media. Search LinkedIn or other places to identify your marketing tribe candidates. Create and try multiple email and LinkedIn messages to invite people to your group. When inviting people, focus on the benefits of being part of the marketing tribe and what you are willing to do to help them.

Tribe Member Requests

You can ask your marketing tribe members questions, ask for recommendations, and utilize members to publish or engage with your book marketing media. The success of getting your marketing tribe members to help you depends on what activities you ask them to do, how you ask them, and how often you send requests. When sending requests, keep them short, simple, and provide your tribe members with specific instructions, links, and ready to use sample materials.

For example: Email Subject Line: Quick Request, <media post topic>. Hi John, Can you please publish this post or something similar on my discussion group: "Ready to publish media post text" and Link to Group - <link>. Happy to help you in return.

This request would take John about 60 seconds to complete if he uses your suggested media post. It also adds value to John's online influence as it is additional topic related media published by him.

Member Rewards

Marketing tribe member key rewards include publicity, credibility, and backlinks. Offer to promote your members on your media channels— Twitter, Blog, Facebook, etc. in return for them helping you. Because marketing tribe members get and publish more media posts by being part of the group, they are more discoverable for that topic.

Member Tracking

Setup a spreadsheet or database that lists each marketing tribe member. Track what requests you sent and when you sent them along with the data and the URL for when your tribe member completed your request. You can send 1- 3 request reminders over several weeks. Members who do not respond or complete requests should be identified and not contacted again.

Online Retail Book Pre-Orders

Books in development can be listed for pre-order sales on retail sites such as Amazon and other online stores. Making books available for pre-orders can be a great way to develop awareness, get credibility, and make new connection contacts for reviewers. Listing a book as available for pre-order can help to motivate the author to complete the book.

Online Retail Book Pre-Orders

- Retail Book URL(s)
- Cover & Description
- Keywords & Categories
- Future Release Date
- Pre-Release Version
- Initial Purchases

© Lawrence Harte, 2019-2020

Book Retail URL(s)

After your book has been setup for pre-orders by online retailers (Amazon, Kobo, etc.), they will publish a web page which provides you with a URL that you can use to promote the book. Having an Amazon or other online retailer book URL provides you with credibility (the book is real) and a simple way to share future book information.

Cover

Your book cover is one of the most important influencers for your book buyers. Create a cover that gets attention, develops interest, and provides credibility. It is possible to start with a basic cover so you can get your online store listing and URL. You can change/update your book cover image until a few days before the scheduled release.

Description

The purpose of a book description is to help the reader understand and feel the value they will get from buying your book. Describe the key topics and benefits the reader will get from reading the book. For non-fiction books this is the problems your book will solve. For fiction books, this is the key challenge the story deals with (the "hook"). Include special features and information that will help the reader understand why the book will help them (social proof). Include key book topic search words and phrases in the description.

Categories

To select your book categories, find similar books, make a list of their categories, and review those categories to determine the top selling book in each category. Go to Amazon.com, select best sellers, select the categories from your list, and look at the sales rank of the top selling books in that category. Top category selling books that are not popular on Amazon (low sales rank) indicate that that category does not have much competition. Picking at least one category with a limited number of competing books increases the likelihood that the book will achieve #1 best seller status for that category when it is launched.

Future Release Date

Pick a future publication date that is realistic. The penalty for missing a future publication date on Amazon and other online stores can range from not being allowed to setup future book pre-orders for a year to delisting your book.

Pre-Release Version

Include a partial pre-release version of your book that can be immediately downloaded. In your online retail store pre-release version (you may have multiple pre-release versions), include links to additional resources that book buyers can visit for more information. Include offers on your resources pages that motivate pre-sale book buyers to go to and share their contact information with you—list building. Do not put download offer links directly in the pre-release version of your book as this may violate the terms of service of the online retailer.

Author and Book Profile Pages

Creating or claiming your author profile pages on online book retailers, book directories and review sites such as BookBub can be a great way to develop online awareness, credibility, and share information and updates about your book.

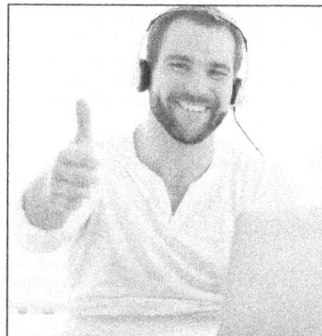

Author and Book Profile Pages

- **Book Directory and Review Sites**
- **Author Profile**
- **Book Profile**
- **Notifications**
- **Advance Review Copies (ARCs)**

© Lawrence Harte, 2019-2020

Book Directory and Review Sites

There are many book directories and review sites that list books and allow people to discover and post feedback and reviews about the books. There are a mix of paid directories, professional review services, and library book listing services. Make a list of the top book directories and submit your book and descriptions to them.

Author Profiles

You can setup author profiles on some online stores, book directories, and other book media platforms. Some online stores automatically create author profile pages (such as Amazon Central) that need to be claimed by authors. After you have claimed and setup your author profiles, you can add your book list along with additional information. Your author profile can include your story along with experiences that add credibility to your books. Make a list of your author profiles and keep track what you provided and when you updated them.

NOTE that you will not have a page on Amazon until your book is available there.

Book Profile Pages

Add your book to multiple book directory and review sites including BookBub, Kobo, and others. Create a description that focuses on the benefits the book will provide. Put your most important benefits in the first 50 words of your description. You may want to have multiple book descriptions with different keywords and highlights to enable the search engines to index your book for multiple topics that your book covers. Include blurbs and quotes to build value and credibility. Use your marketing tribe to post initial reviews and comments about your book on these sites. Periodically ask happy readers to post reviews.

Book Blurbs

Get 3+ book blurb quotes about the value of a book from topic leaders, influencers, and other authors. In addition to adding credibility to your book with value statements from key trusted influencers, you are likely to make new connections with key influencers who may help you in many ways.

Book Blurb Candidate List

Start by making a list of topic leaders, influencers, and/or authors you want to get book blurbs from. Review their profiles and find their achievements related to your book topic. Review some of their articles, books, or media they have published. Your initial goal is to ask to develop a relationship connection. You can follow up with a blurb request after they learn about you and why they should trust and help you. Send a request message for help with your book topic. Reference something that they have achieved related to your book as the reason you have asked for their help.

Book Blurb Message

Your book blurb messages should be a value statement and an endorsement. Make a list of the key values for your book that your readers need or desire. Review book blurbs from competing or similar books. Create sample book blurbs you would like to have.

Book Blurb Exchange Request

Send a book blurb exchange request message to your blurb candidate after you have developed some relationship trust and value with them. Provide a sample blurb and some suggested keywords if they want to write their own blurb. Offer to swap book blurbs or to provide some other value in exchange for them helping you. Include a link to your book or offer an advance copy of your book if they want it.

Online Discussion Groups

Online discussion groups are good places to discover key book-related topics, find and connect with experts and key influencers, and publish information that helps people to discover and purchase your book.

Book Promo & Online Discussion Groups

- Discussion Topics & Keywords
- Group Ownership
- Group Building
- Group Moderation
- Indirect Book Promotion

Important Topics, Trusted Expert, Keywords, Topic Challenges

© Lawrence Harte, 2019-2020

Discussion Topics & Keywords

Join several book-related topic discussion groups, learn key topics, words, and phrases members use and respond to. Make lists of important topics, phrases, and keywords. You can use these in your promotional materials and media posts. Learn what topics are popular (many likes and shares) and the types of comments they get.

Group Ownership

Set up and run your own group after you have monitored and engaged with other groups. Group ownership on LinkedIn, Facebook, Reddit, and other discussion platforms is usually free. Owning and leading a group provides you with authority, credibility, and influencer power. By owning a group, you will think like an owner which will help you to understand what is acceptable to publish and contribute to other groups you have joined.

Group Building

Build your group in three key phases; first, get 50+ people to join so that potential new members see that there are people in the group. In phase two, get 50+ more members that are qualified and give them ready to publish posts that cover key topics. This will help potential new members to see valuable activity. In phase three, recruit and invite qualified members and help them to publish valuable posts in your group.

Group Moderation

It is important to monitor group discussions and comments in your group to determine if they are acceptable for the group. If someone posts something inappropriate or is doing self-promotion, quickly remove the post, contact the contributor, let them know the topic requirements, and ask them to resubmit the post that fits your groups topic requirements. You can share or transfer your group moderation role to co-organizers and members.

Indirect Book Promotion

The terms of service of discussion groups typically do not allow direct promotion of books or other products. To promote your book, you should use indirect promotion. You can do indirect promotion by asking questions about book topics, sharing tips covered in your book, or asking for help with topics or stories that are in your book. You can ask your marketing tribe to post comments on your group discussion posts asking about your experience which may allow you to mention your book.

Book Blog

A book blog can be used to publish discoverable topic related information that attracts potential book buyers, develops value and credibility, and recommends an action or provides additional resources. Key types of book blog posts include book-related topic questions and answers, resource lists, guides, and other related information.

Blog Purpose

The purposes of a book blog include enabling topic discovery (search engine), content sharing, and social engagement. Blog posts are discoverable by search engines, so it is good to include keywords and phrases in the blog post title and in the content. Blog posts content can share messages and information that relate to your book. Blog posts can be used as social engagement when you allow comments. Unfortunately, enabling comments on blog posts may get many spam comments. It may be better to encourage responses to blog posts through a web page form which can eliminate most automatic spam comment submissions.

Blog Post Types

Blog posts can be grouped into categories of purpose, content, and formats. The type of blog post relates to its discoverability, influence, and buying intent of the reader. List posts identify tools, services, and other items. People tend to search for lists when they are in the buying phase. For example, people who search for "Top Book Launch Marketing Books" tend to be looking for book marketing help. Guide and checklist blog posts provide how-to instructions for people who are in the implementation phase of their project. Infographics are visual explanations of how something works. Guest posts share information from other people (experts and influencers) which can help authors to make new connections while getting blog content value. Research posts provide key data and hard to find information. People who are searching for research data may be looking to justify a project or purchase. News and announcement posts share recent information about a topic. Because news and announcements provide only temporary value, including news in blog posts can make your blog look very outdated when viewed months or years later.

Blog Post Images

Blog posts should usually include photos or other media to get the attention of the viewer. The image content should be related to the blog message and it should look good when it is in small size because many blog readers will use their smartphones with small screens. It can be helpful if the image displayed is useful and benefits the blog post topic.

Blog Post Templates

Blog post templates can be used to create more effective blog posts faster. Start by creating a templates file where you can store, find, and copy templates. Group the templates into categories such as lists, guides, research, news, and other formats. To create the templates, create original posts and convert them into generic versions with replaceable tags.

Blog Post Call to Action

Most blog posts should contain a follow-up call to action (CTA) that the reader can take. This follow-up action should provide some additional value to the message. The CTA is typically a link to a resource or offer such as a discount for the book.

Blog Post Schedule

The schedule you should setup for book blog posting depends on how you will use your blog. If your blog is setup for social sharing (community), it is important to publish information at regular intervals (daily, weekly, etc.). If your blog is primarily used to share discoverable content, it is okay to publish on an irregular schedule.

Book Image Marketing

Book images (cover, interior, and related images) can be published with search engine discoverable titles, descriptions, and links that attract and motivate people to discover and buy your book and related products or services. Images can be quickly grouped into image boards (topics) and icons and links can be added (overlaid) to the images allowing them to be seen and used when people share them (legally or unauthorized). Create short descriptions for each photo along with a link where they can get additional information and/or buy the book.

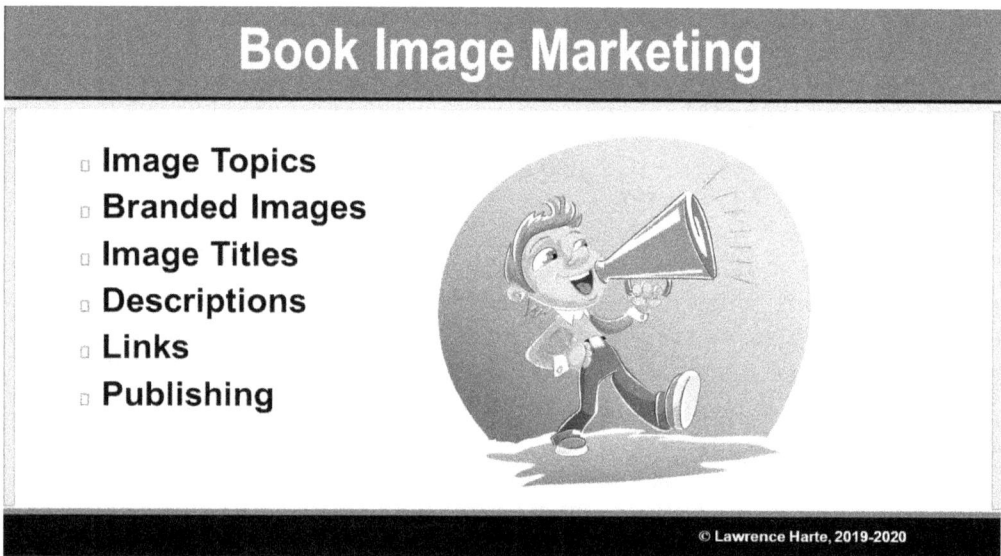

© Lawrence Harte, 2019-2020

Image List

You should have an image list spreadsheet or database file that includes image information, category ids, and links to image media. Have images in multiple sizes (portrait, horizontal) and formats (pdf, jpg, etc), and use the size in the item file name (e.g. cover_2560x1600 - for Amazon). Also include links to each version of image.

Image Titles

A key value of your images is your discoverable and influential title. Use keywords that are search discoverable for book-related topic keywords and categories. Include words that stimulate emotion and help the person to understand and feel the benefit of the image.

Image Descriptions

Images descriptions start with a statement that helps their targeted audiences to understand the purpose or value of the image. Include trigger keywords and buying motivators to develop emotions, interest, and desire. Finish with a value statement or recommended call to action (CTA).

Image Links

Copy the published URL of each image and add it to your image list. Create destination URLs that people go to when they click on your image. You can include this link in the image description. You may also include the destination URL in the image graphic to ensure viewers see your destination URL. Some image sharing sites may hide the destination URL in the description. Including the destination URL in the image graphic also ensures people will see your URL when they copy and share the image without the image description.

Image Sharing Platforms

Set up one or more image sharing services such as Pinterest, Instagram, or others. Create discoverable titles which can be found on the platform and in search engines. If possible, group images together into categories such as boards on Pinterest.

Image Creation

You can use simple image creation tools such as Canva to create basic images. To get multiple concepts, use design contests such as 99Designs.com or Freelancer.com. Design contests usually allow you to run polls to determine which images are the best choice. Include your logo, URL, or some branding style in your images. Including your brand will allow people to identify your media when it is copied and shared without descriptions. It is important to get permissions to use images. You can get images with unrestricted rights from Pixels or Pixabay. Be careful when using images from design contests. Designers may use unauthorized copies of images and trademarks in their designs.

Book Video Marketing

Book content and related information can be converted into short videos with searchable titles, engaging descriptions, and links to your book and related services. Videos can be quickly created using images with effects (fade in/out) and moving text that allows viewers to get value with or without audio. Video clips can be grouped into channels that cover specific book related topics. Messages, icons, and links can be added (overlaid) to your video allowing them to be seen and used when people share them (legally or unauthorized). Create short descriptions for each video along with a link where they can get additional information and/or buy the book.

Book Video Marketing

- Video Types
- Branded Videos
- Video Titles
- Descriptions
- Links
- Publishing

© Lawrence Harte, 2019-2020

Video Types

Key book marketing video types include book trailers (topic teaser), guides, webinars and interviews, reviews, and video FAQs. Book trailers are usually 1-3 minute book benefit descriptions. The trailer should focus on what the viewer can do or will feel after reading the book. Book trailers usually include an image of book cover, images that help the reader to discover the topic and needs, and includes a solution or satisfaction promise at the end. Guides and instruction videos help the viewer to understand how to do something. The guide video can be a video recording during a teaching activity, screen activities (screencasts), or other media that helps the reader to understand steps and how to do them. Webinars and interviews allow experts to discuss book related topics. Inviting experts to be on a webinar or to be interviewed has high connection values. One webinar or interview can be divided into multiple videos. Reviews are evaluations and opinions on the value of products or items. People tend to search for reviews when they are in the final buying stages. Video frequently ask questions (VFAQs) are simple recordings of questions and nswers. While there is little value added by making questions and answers in video format, there is high search engine discovery value.

Video Titles

A key value of your book videos are their search discoverable and influential titles. Use a mixture of book topic and emotional benefit keywords. You may want to create multiple versions of your videos that use different titles with alternative keywords.

Video Descriptions

Video descriptions are actually benefit descriptions because they describe the solutions or satisfactions the viewer gets by watching them. The description starts with a statement that helps qualified audiences understand how the video relates to their needs and interests. If the viewer can relate to the first line of the description (qualification), they continue reading the description (or start to watch the video.) The description body should include trigger keywords and buying motivators to develop emotions, interest, and desire. The end of the description should have a value statement or recommended call to action (CTA).

Video Links

Copy the published URL of each video and add it to your video list. Create destination URLs that people go to when they click on your video. You can include this link in the video description. You may also include the destination URL in the video content to ensure viewers see your destination URL. Some video sharing platforms hide the destination URL in the description.

Video Sharing Platforms

Set up one or more video sharing services such as Youtube, Vimeo, or others. Create discoverable titles which can be found on the platform and in search engines. Set up a video channel which people can subscribe to and get alerts as you release new videos.

Video Production

You can use ready to edit video templates, simple image creation tools such as wevideo.com, more powerful video editing software such as Adobe Premier, or have other people such as online projects or local contractors create your videos. The first 30-60 seconds of your video is most important as most people don't view past 60-90 seconds. Create no lingual videos if possible (self-explaining images and icons). Many people will watch the video without sound.

You can use ready-made stock video to save production time and cost. It is important to get permissions to use images, sound, and video clips. You can stock video clips with unrestricted rights from pexels.com, free audio and music clips from ccmixter.org, and free audio sound effects from freesound.org. Be careful when creating videos using online projects. Freelancers may use unauthorized copies of images, videos, and trademarks in media and not tell you.

Include your logo, destination URL, or some branding style in your video content. Including it in your video media will allow people to identify your media when it is copied and shared without descriptions.

Book Crowdfunding Campaigns

Book crowdfunding campaigns are online financial contribution projects that allow people to donate or order rewards to help a book project. In addition to getting money for a book project, crowdfunding projects can be a great way to develop awareness, sell books, get sales leads and get book reviewers. You can do crowdfunding campaigns before, during, and after your book is released. Crowdfunding campaigns can be set up and run on platforms such as Kickstarter, Indiegogo, and others.

Book Crowdfunding Campaigns

- Publicity
- Credibility
- Feedback
- Contact List
- Rewards
- Pre-Sales
- Risks

© Lawrence Harte, 2019-2020

Crowdfunding Benefits

Crowdfunding campaigns can generate money, publicity, and make new contacts. Crowdfunding money can come from goodwill contributions, book purchases, sponsorships, and other rewards. Crowdfunding campaigns tend to get rapidly listed high in search engine results during and long after your campaign is over. This provides publicity and may allow you to earn money while promoting your book and related services. People who donate to get items from you such as your book, logo items, and services can become new connections. Some of these new connections can be great sources of books development help (interviews) and book reviews.

Crowdfunding Types

The type of crowdfunding platform can dramatically determine how willing people are to contribute, how much money you get (the percentage they keep), and the amount of risk you take if your campaign is not successful. Using well-known crowdfunding services such as Kickstarter and Indiegogo tend to have a higher trust level with contributors. Fixed crowdfunding projects require you reach your target or you don't get any money. Flexible crowdfunding campaigns allow you to keep any contributed money even if you miss your goal. The key difference is flex funding projects take a higher percentage of the donations. A key risk for doing crowdfunding projects is risk of failure. If you cancel your project or don't hit your goal, the fundraising platform will show it. These "cancelled" pages tend to stay in the search results which can confuse people who are looking to buy your book and find a web page that says "Cancelled."

Project Description

Your crowdfunding project should describe what the project is, why it is important to contributors, and what they get for contributing. Describe the challenge or reason why you are developing your book and how people will benefit from it. Explain what you need to achieve your project goals. Include a link to a sample or resource about your book crowdfunding project. Your description should be an emotional appeal about the value or benefits of your book.

Reward List

Crowdfunding campaigns usually include a list of rewards contributors get according to the amount of the donation. Book crowdfunding rewards can range from a thank you message on your book website (e.g. $5) to a book authoring project ($5,000+). Review crowdfunding descriptions of similar books and see the types of rewards they are providing. Follow up with contributors who donate enough to get your book. These people can be great advance copy reviewers and are likely to post good book reviews on Amazon and other sites.

Invite List

While some crowdfunding campaigns may get donations from unknown people, most crowdfunding projects require personal invites and very active promotion to get contributors. Create a list (spreadsheet or database) of family, friends, associates, and others that you can use to track when you sent initial requests, follow up requests, and when the person contributed. It is important to get a lot of people to contribute in the first 1-2 days so your project will get shown to more people on the contribution platform.

Inviting

Inviting contributions involves sending initial requests and motivational follow up messages. Create sample invite and follow up messages for the types of people you invite (family friends, associates, connections, etc.). Personalizing invite messages helps people to understand it is not an automatic request which can dramatically increase your success rate. Key request communication options include email, social network connections, and phone. If you use social network connections (messaging), there may be a delay in response. Be prepared to ask 2-3 times even for a small contribution and send separate follow up requests by 3+ days.

Book Pre-Launch Sponsorships

Offering book pre-launch sponsorships are good ways for authors, publishers, and marketers to develop book awareness and to get money or value for inserting media into a book and its promotional media.

Book Pre-Launch Sponsorships

- Sponsorship Types
- In Book Media & Links
- Media Posts with Links
- Content Rules

SPONSOR

© Lawrence Harte, 2019-2020

Book sponsorships can earn money or some other value such as promotion or service bartering. It can be much easier to convince a company or person to become a sponsor if they agree to provide promotion value (barter) in return for the sponsorship option. The sponsor could agree to publish several blog posts and Tweets about the book. Consider the deal between the Universal Pictures and Mars company for the agreement to use Reece's Pieces as a candy item in the movie ET. The agreement was for Mars candies to spend $1 million dollars on promotion of the movie in return for their featured candy. It is estimated Reece's Pieces earned an extra $20M from the movie promotion. Hershey's was the first choice with M&Ms. Hershey's said no.

Sponsorship Types

Book pre-launch sponsorship types can include content, media, and contacts. Content sponsorships insert content or include references to screen shots, guides, or other helpful information in the book. Media sponsorships include sponsor company or product references in media posts and other book promotional materials. Media posts include links that can provide search engine value to the sponsor. Contact sponsorship is the providing of information about people who register to get materials paid for by the sponsor (free book). It is important to let the purchasers know that their contact information is being provided to the sponsor when they choose to get their book for free.

In Book Media

In book media sponsorships allow companies or people to include an image (screen shot), logo, text, or other content in the book. This can be screen shots, information and/or other media, and/or links to additional references. Send a final layout version of the book pages that contain the sponsor's content to get their approval. It can be very bad if there is a typo or other error and the book has been released.

In-Book Sponsor Links

In-book sponsor links allow readers to get additional information from a sponsor's website. This may be a resource, template, or other valuable information mentioned in the book in an appropriate section. The in-book sponsor link should be in URL (and clickable text format in Ebooks). Links in books should be redirected to their destination through the author or publisher websites. This will allow the link to be redirected if the sponsor company goes out of business or the content on their sponsored destination page becomes inappropriate.

Media Posts

Sponsors can pay to have their content and links included in book blog posts, tweets, images, and/or videos. You can set the number of media posts and types they will sponsor. The media posts can say "sponsored by" and include a link to the sponsor's website. Getting multiple backlinks from topic related media sites and channels can provide significant search value to the sponsor. It is important to sell content sponsorships and not to offer links for sale. Search engines have restrictions on selling links.

Sponsored Content Rules

Create sponsor content rules that define appropriate content and restrictions. For example, unjustified claims or bad comments about competitors may not be allowed. Sponsored media and resources should be helpful for the user. This allows you to earn sponsorship money by providing more value to your readers.

Book Acknowledgments

Including a book acknowledgments section in your book can be a great way to get credibility, book reviews, and get influencers to help promote your book.

Book Acknowledgements

- **Acknowledgement List**
- **Book Page Text**
- **Sample Books**
- **Book Review Request**

Book Acknowledgment List

Make a list of people who helped you with the creation of the book. They can be anyone including developers, reviewers, contributors, and people that inspired you. They do not have to know you or have participated in the development to be included in your acknowledgment list.

Acknowledgment Book Text

Include the person's name and company name if possible in the acknowledgment section (example - Bob Smith with IBM). Alphabetically sort names in your acknowledgement text which can help to avoid people feeling prioritized or snubbed. You can group people into categories such as "Special thanks to people from cloud service providers including:"

Sample Book

When your book is completed, send a sample copy with a thankful inscription with something you admire or respect about them. Insert a sticky note to the acknowledgment page with an arrow that points to their name in the book. Include a cover letter for the sample book thanking them.

Book Review Request

Ask for a book review request about 1 to 4 weeks after you send the sample book. Send the request to post a book review on Amazon and other review websites and include a link to the book on the website to make it easy for them. You can suggest keywords to use in the book review to make it easier to write the review and keywords that search engines can find.

Book Pre-Launch for Job & New Clients

Book development activities can be used to get a new job or new projects. Even if you don't finish the book, the book development process can get you job interviews or new business clients. Start by making connections at companies by requesting media items for your book from marketing communications people. Develop and expand your media relationship to other people in the company. After you develop your new company contact relationships, ask about their company and if they need help with projects.

Book Pre-Launch for Job & New Clients

- **Media Request**
- **Expert Help**
- **Company Connections**
- **Job or Project Requests**

YOU ARE HIRED!

© Lawrence Harte, 2019-2020

Job resumes are disqualification tools. Companies receive hundreds or thousands of job resumes. They don't have time to look at qualifications, they focus on finding things that disqualify.

You can bypass much of the job application and resume process by getting recommended for a job or a project by someone inside the company. Some companies even pay people a bonus for recommending new hires. The key is making contacts inside the company and helping that person to understand that you are a great fit for their company. If you make a new company contact as part of your book development, the person knows that you are qualified and knowledgeable because you are the one that wrote the book on it!

Media Requests

Develop your first contacts at the company by requesting media items (photos, content) for your book. Get a company press release, request a media item from the press contact. The marketing contacts are paid to get publicity for their company and they want to help you.

New Company Connections

Ask your media contact for a referral inside the company to help with book development or directly contact other people in the company mentioning that you are working with the media person. Use the media person's name for credibility (name dropping).

Start a relationship with your new contact by asking short and simple questions related to your book. Limit your initial communication. Connect with them on LinkedIn and endorse them for skills related to their job. Offer to co-author an article with your contact (few usually accept) and ask what you can do to help them in return for them helping you.

Expert Help Request

Ask your new connection to review a short section of your book. Offer to include their name in the book if they help you. Send them a short section of your book (3-10 pages).

Job or Project Request

After you have developed a relationship with your company contact, thank them for helping and send a request to learn if they or someone else at their company needs help with projects. Mention something about their company that you admire in the request. Do not mention a job or payment for projects. The main purpose is to get you to discover a potential opportunity related to your skills and experience.

Book Pre-Launch Advertising

Good book advertising sends book promotion information to people who have an interest in your book (targeting). Review ad campaigns from similar books, use their ads and targeting to help set up your ad campaigns.

Sample Ads

To speed up and improve your book advertising results, search and review sample ads for similar books. Search for your book like your audience is likely to search, copy sample ads, use them to create ad templates for your book. Use the templates to create muliple ads for your book.

Ad Keywords

The typical book marketing ad campaign uses book-related topic keywords to trigger the insertion and display of ads. Make a master list of ad keywords using a combination of your book topic knowledge and the keywords the advertising system recommends for you. Group your ad keywords with ad messages/media that you have created. Continually test keywords and ad combinations to find which combinations work best. Some book ad platforms (such as Amazon Marketing Services - AMS) can automatically create ads and select keywords for you. Automatic ads may be a good way to start but you may be able to find or improve on the results with your own keywords and ads. You can also identify negative keywords which stop your ads from showing. For example, adding the negative keyword "free" will keep your ads from appearing when people search for books with "free" in their search phrase.

Ad Platforms

There are multiple book advertising platform options. Set up multiple book advertising accounts on online bookstores (Amazon), directories (BookBub), and other places that people would react well to ads for your book.

Ad Campaigns

Set up and run multiple book ad campaigns with limited budgets starting 1-2 months before your book release. This will allow you to learn how to do advertising with little risk and very low cost. Review and learn which keywords and ads produce the best results. About one week prior to your book campaign, increase the budget on your most successful campaigns.

#1 Best Seller Book Launch

To get #1 Best Seller Status on Amazon during launch (it is easier than you think), you need to have a good book cover graphic, motivational description, pick the right book categories, get influencers to mention your book, do pre-sales promotion, offer a book launch bonus, and test and optimize book advertising.

Book Cover

You should have a book cover that gets attention, develops interest, and creates confidence that it directly relates to the book topic. Your book should stand out (pop) when grouped with other book covers of similar topic areas. This can be accomplished with color, shapes, or images. Your cover media should develop interest in the book topic. Interest can be developed from benefit application images (experiencing the book topic), book topic icons, and topic trigger keywords. Your cover should appear credible and have a well-thought-out design that builds trust. If the cover looks amateurish or has a haphazard layout, viewers may believe that the content inside the book is also amateurish. Launch your pre-order versions early even if your cover is not the best. Use the feedback to create a better cover. You can upload new versions of your cover before the book is released.

Book Description

Book descriptions start with a statement (first line) that helps their desired audiences to identify something they need (problem to solve) or want (emotional desire). Include trigger keywords and buying motivators to develop emotions, interest, and desire. Finish with a value statement (solution promise).

Category Selection

Books can get #1 ranking status in their categories which are reviewed over time periods (hours or days). Some book categories have limited competition which can make it relatively easy to get best seller status with a small number of book sales. Select book topic related categories which have relatively low sales for your book topic.

Influencer Marketing

You can get a lot of publicity and credibility by getting influencers to mention, comment, and share information about your future book to their followers. Search for your book topic and make a list of people who have followers that trust them (book authors, podcasters, and others).

Start by making a connection with an influencer by sending a question about something they have done, asking for help with a topic they have experience with, or some other request that demonstrates you know who they are and why they are important. Offer to help them in return for helping you. After you have made the connection and set up a trusted relationship, you can then ask for help to promote your book. Create ready to publish media posts that reference your book and ask them to publish it as a guest post on your blog. You are giving them publicity while they are helping you. You can then ask them to mention you or your book on their media channels - Twitter, Blog, YouTube.

Book Launch Bonus

Create pre-sales offers that provide incentives to people who pre-purchase your book. This can be a guide, tips, or a related story. Create a pre-release partial version of your book that is available for immediate download.

Pre-Sales List

To get sales on launch day, start to do promotion weeks or months before your book and develop a pre-sales list. Add them to your email list. Send a book launch reminder the day before and an "Finally Here Available Now" message with a link to where they can buy the book. You can ask the book buyer to send you an image of their purchase screen to get their bonus reward.

Advertising

Advertising for pre-orders can generate awareness, influence, and sales for people who don't know you or your book (yet). Advertise on multiple book platforms including Amazon, Kobo, BookBub, and others. Find sample ads and the keywords that trigger the ads and use them as examples for your book ads and campaign targeting. Run low budget test ad campaigns for 1-3 months before book launch to discover effective ads and keywords. Increase your ad budget 3-5 days before the release of your book.

Marketing Campaign Success To-Do List

Learn book marketing options to get a big picture of 20+ campaign options and the key skills & resources they require.

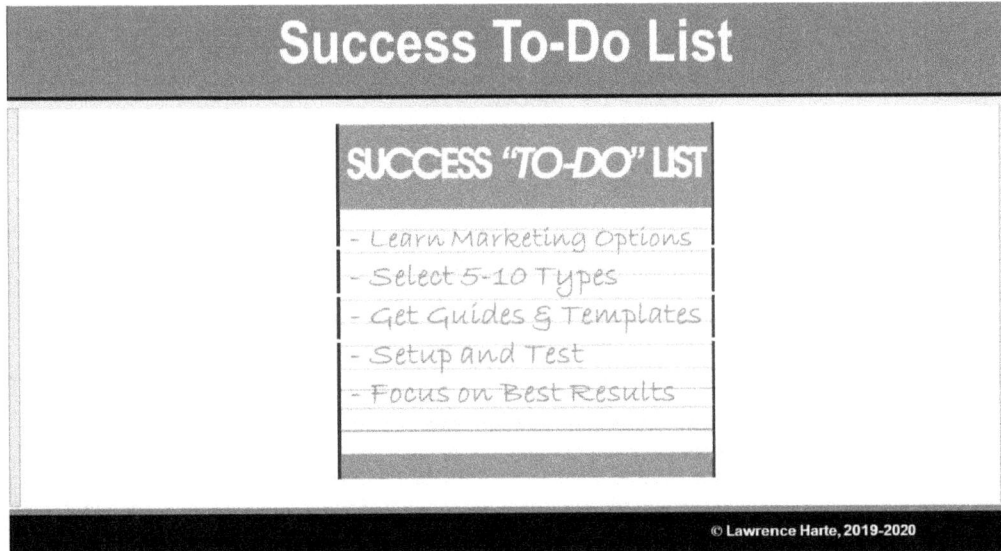

Select Marketing Types

Choose 5-10 types of book marketing that have a good fit for your skills, resources, and interests.

Get Guides & Templates

Get sample book marketing processes, guides, and templates. Update and adapt them to your files, tools, and services.

Set up & Test

Set up, test, and continually adapt/optimize multiple book marketing campaigns for 2-3 months.

Focus on Effective Marketing Types

After your initial tests, shift most of your book efforts to the top 3-5 marketing activities that get good results.

Appendix 1 - Book Pre-Launch Marketing Resources

This is a list of resources for the Book Pre-Launch Marketing Course and Book. These resources help authors, marketers, and others involved in book promotion to get publicity, credibility, and earn money before publishing their book.

Get access to 100+ downloadable and editable guides, sample plans, templates, and other media items along with instructions and sample materials.

To get access to these materials, go to:

LearnQIC.com/bookprelaunchresources

Book Pre-Launch Marketing Plan - Objectives, Book Details, Audiences, Media Channels, Media Items, Key Activities, and Resources.

Book Pre-Launch Marketing Master Task List - Spreadsheet that describes 100+ book pre-launch promotion activities, priority, resource link, and responsibility.

Book Pre-Launch Marketing Checklist – One-page sheet that lists key book pre-launch marketing activities.

Book Marketing Media Channels - Spreadsheet that lists 20+ typical promotion channels (Twitter, Blog, Facebook, Pinterest, Quora, etc), name, URL, purpose, strategies, & recommended posting schedule.

Book Pre-Launch Marketing Procedures - Sample steps and processes on how to do marketing campaigns, projects, and tasks.

Book Buyer Interview Guide - How to find and talk to candidate book readers to discover key topics, activities, & media channels for more effective promotion.

Book Blog Post Templates - Templates for 8+ types of book blog posts.

Book Press Release Sample - Sample book announcement press release for media & consumers.

Book Business Card Template - Sample layout of two-sided book business card that shares motivational book info and includes attraction resource for list contact building.

Book Sell Sheet (Brochure) Template - Ready to edit 1-page brochure that helps people and distributors to understand the book value and how they buy it.

Book Sponsorship Agreement Template - Sample agreement for that allows a promoter to pay for book content insertion, book give away (sponsors get contact info), and/or promotional media messages with backlinks.

Book Crowdfunding Guide - Steps to set up and run book crowdfunding campaigns for publicity, book pre-sales, and to get other money.

Book Crowdfunding Campaign Rewards - List and description of key items (books, services, +) that can be provided to people for their contributions.

Contribution and Use Permission Forms - Sample agreement document which provides written verification to use contributed photos and materials in your book.

Online Book Retailer Pre-Order Setup Guide - Steps to set up a book for presales on Amazon and other online bookstores.

Appendix 2 - Book Pre-Launch Marketing Guides

This is a list of guides for the Book Pre-Launch Marketing Course & Book. These guides help authors, marketers, and others involved in book promotion to get publicity, credibility, and earn money before publishing their book.

Get access to 100+ downloadable and editable guides, sample plans, templates, and other media items along with instructions and sample materials.

To get access to these materials, go to:

LearnQIC.com/bookprelaunchguides

Book Media Channels - Steps to find and set up 10+ key media accounts and profiles (Blog, Facebook, Reddit, etc.) for sending and sharing book promotion messages.

Book Brochure Creation Guide - Instruction on how to edit a one-page brochure (template provided) that helps people and distributors to understand the book value and how they buy it.

Book Buyer Interview Guide - How to find and talk to candidate book readers to discover key topics, activities, and media channels for more effective promotion.

Book Blog Guide - How to set up a book blog, effective blog post types, and how to create and publish on your blog.

Pre-Release Book Creation Guide - Steps and resources to create a partial version of a book for pre-sales orders (purchase incentives) and key motivational resources to include.

Book Sponsorship Sales Guide - Instructions on how to offer and sell content and registration sponsorships before releasing your book.

Book Crowdfunding Guide - Steps to set up and run book crowdfunding campaigns for publicity, book pre-sales, and to get other money.

Contribution and Use Permission Form Guide - Steps to request and get written verification to use contributed photos and materials in your book.

Online Book Retailer Pre-Order Setup Guide - Steps to set up a book for presales on Amazon and other online bookstores.

Book Media Contributors Guide - How to find and get people to provide photos and media to use in your book.

#1 Amazon Best Seller Status Guide - Steps to pick the right book categories, get influencers to mention your book, pre-sales promotion, book launch bonus, and book advertising testing & optimization.

Appendix 3 - Book Pre-Launch Marketing Tips

This is a list of tips for the Book Pre-Launch Marketing Course and Book. These resources help authors, marketers, and others involved in book promotion to get publicity, credibility, and earn money before publishing their book.

To get access to these materials, go to:

LearnQIC.com/bookprelaunchtips

Book Business Card and Script - Create a book business card that includes book cover image, top three buying motivators, topic trigger words (on back), and attraction resources (motivate contact submission).

Get Photo and Media Contributors - Find press releases related to your book topic, contact the media people at the bottom of the press release, and ask them for photos and media content to use in our book. Public relations people are paid to help you.

Book Content Sponsorships - Offer to include content from people or companies inside your book in return for money or other value such as promotion messages. Set up guidelines to ensure the content is helpful to your book readers.

Book Crowdfunding Campaigns for Publicity – Set up a crowdfunding campaign for your book. Offer multiple rewards (gifts) including your book and media promotion options. A key benefit is that crowdfunding campaigns rapidly show up high in search engine results pages.

Book Pre-Release Buyer Interviews - Create an offer in the pre-release version of your book such as a free guide or resource to motivate people to register. Contact these people and do book buyer journey interviews to learn why and how they buy books like yours.

Book Dominant Buying Motivators (DBMs) - Identify book buying motivators from book buyer journey interviews. Review and identify the top three book DBMs and use them in promo materials, media posts, and in discussions with readers and fans.

Start Book Topic Online Groups - Create online groups that cover your book topic. Use your book title as part of the group name.

Online Book Topic Discussion Group Post Seeding - Create 20+ high topic value discussion posts for your new group, over 1-2 months, invite influencers to join your discussion group and offer a ready to publish discussion for them to post. Offer that you and your marketing team will like and share the post (social value).

Book Blurb Exchanges - Contact authors of related books and offer to exchange book blurb endorsement comments. Review their book information before contacting them and find something to praise in the invite message you send.

Email List Access Bartering - Offer to provide access to your book buyer and reader contact list to share a value item (such as a free story, guide or template) in return for access to their contact list.

Book Pre-Release Version(s) with Downloadable Resources - Create a partial pre-release version of your book that includes value downloadable resources that allow you to capture contact information (list building).

Book Amazon Affiliate Link(s) – Set up an Amazon affiliate account and insert your book product page into your website, blog, and other media. This allows you to earn additional referral sales commissions on orders for your book and anything else the person buys on Amazon after they click your affiliate link.

Get Sample Book Media Posts - Search like your readers and gather sample media posts for related books and content. Use these (the popular ones) as a guide to create your book marketing media posts.

If you have a book pre-launch marketing tip to share or an update to suggest, submit at:

https://LearnQIC.com/bookprelaunchsubmit

For your submission, you will be listed as a sponsor and receive a link to your website.

Appendix 4 - Book Pre-Launch Marketing Checklist

Book Pre-Launch Marketing Checklist

Sample

Marketing Management:
Marketing Plan:
Master Task List
Document Index
Media Files & Templates
Procedures
Media Item List

Book Research:
Competitive Analysis
Media Contributors
Reader Interviews
Sharable Resources
Questions & Answers
Tips & Stories

Promo Materials:
Descriptions - 25-500+ words
Keywords - Primary, Secondary
Buying Motivators (DBMs)
Book Story - Why Important
Cover Image - Design Contest
Book Logos - Small Graphics
Press Release - Value, Features
Book Web Page
Book Business Card
Book Brochure - Sales Sheet
Book Press Kit
Book Pre-Release Version(s)

Media Channels:
Media Channel List
Media Channel Setup
Social Profiles - 10+

Media Posts:
Gather Samples
Media Posts - Content Sources
Media Post Templates
Editorial Calendar

Marketing Campaigns:
List Management
Book Contributors - 20+
Marketing Tribe - 10+
Online Pre-Orders - Amazon+
Book Profile Pages - Bookbub+
Book Blurbs - 5+
Social Media - 50+ Posts
Online Discussion Groups
Book Blog - 30+ Posts
Book Images - 20+
Book Videos - 5+
Crowdfunding - Publicity+
Book Sponsorships
Book Acknowledgements
Get Job/New Clients
Ad Campaigns
Best Seller Launch

Reward: _____

List Sponsored by: LearnQIC Book Marketing for Authors

LearnQIC.com/bookprelaunchchecklist

Appendix 5 - Book Pre-Launch Marketing Contributions

Do you have a book marketing success tip, resource, guide, case study, or other media that you are willing to share?

Submit your success experience or materials and get Get Publicity, Credibility, and Links.

You can also buy or barter success resource sponsorships for other media (that are not already sponsored yet).

To submit your expert knowledge or resources, go to:

LearnQIC.com/bookprelaunchsubmit

Appendix 6 - Book Marketing Directory

Authors need lists of tools, services, and items that can help them to create, promote, and distribute their books. This book marketing directory is an unbiased and open (no fee) directory.

To get access to these categories and their lists, go to:

LearnQIC.com/bookmarkteingdirectory

Affiliate Networks - List of affiliate networks that authors can use to insert related product offers that earn referral commissions.

Audio Book Distributors - A list of audio book distribution platforms.

Book Advertising Services - A list of services that allow authors and publishers to create, insert, and manage book ads.

Book Angel Funding - A list of companies that provide angel early stage investment for independent publishers.

Book Distribution Platforms - A list of book distribution platforms.

Book Fulfillment Services - A list of platforms or services that can process and deliver book orders.

Book Marketing Podcasts - Online audio and video book marketing podcast shows.

Book Marketing Subscription Service - List of companies or platforms that provide access to books (eBook, Audio book) by a subscription service.

Book Marketing Templates - List of companies, platforms, or services that provide ready to edit book promotional media materials.

Book Promotion Websites - A list of platforms or services that promote books to readers and distributors.

Book Publishing and Sharing Service - List of companies or platforms that provide shared access to books (eBook, Audio book).

Book Review Platforms - List of platforms or services that provide information and reviews about books.

Book Review Services - A list of platforms and services that invite, publish, and manage book reviews.

Crowdfunding Platforms - A list of group funding services that manage contributions for projects.

eBook Distribution Services - A list of ebook distribution platforms.

eBook Production Systems - A list of software or services that are to convert or create eBooks.

Email Service Platforms - A list of email list management platforms that authors can use to manage contact lists and email campaigns.

Link Sharing Platforms - Platforms that assist in the creation and sharing of links on social media networks and other websites.

Online Course Platforms - List of companies or platforms that provide access to online (eLearning) courses.

Print on Demand (POD) - A list of companies that provide book print on demand.

Self-Publishing Platforms - A list of platforms and services that allow book authors to publish and distribute their books.

Index